#BRUH...
Grow Up!

MY GUIDE TO BECOMING A MAN

MsThomasRN
Reproductive Health & Sexuality Educator

HOV
PUBLISHING

#BRUH… Grow Up
My Guide To Becoming A Man

HOV Publishing is a division of HOV, LLC.
www.hovpub.com
email: hopeofvision@gmail.com

Editing & Proofreading: HOV Publishing Editorial Team
Front Cover Design and Inside layout by HOV Design Solutions

To learn more about MsThomasRN's please visit her website at:

ISBN Paperback: 978-1-955107-27-3
ISBN eBook: 978-1-955107-00-6

Printed in the United States of America

To My Baby Boy Maurice,

God showed me you in a dream. I already had a son, and I had a daughter. I was done having children because I had one of each... "a pair". God told me that my purpose in this life was to birth 3 children. He told me that you would come when I least expected it and that you would be a boy. Life before you was challenging, I was trying to navigate through life as a single mom, a working woman and a nursing student all at the same time. Not for one minute did I believe that I would bear another child. After so many years and finally getting my life back on track I was content and living my life in a good place.

I met your dad and after several years of dating we vacationed in Las Vegas. Who knew that you would return with us... because what happened in Vegas did not stay in Vegas... lol. When I found out I was pregnant I cried, not because I didn't want you but because God showed me you in a dream and it came to fruition just like he said it would. Twenty-one years after I had your brother and eighteen years after I had your sister, there you came. From the moment I knew, I had no regrets, and I told God to let his will be done. Now fast forward twelve years later I have watched you go into the handsome young man that you are, and I am so grateful that God paired us together. I don't think I can ever see my life without you. As my youngest child YOU keep me HIGHLY motivated and dedicated to being the best mom to you that I can. You are the reason I continue to work so hard and never expect defeat or failure. In a world where it's so easy to give up, I could have a long time ago, but when I watch you watching me, I say to myself that I have to model what I want you to want for yourself in the future and that's Success! So as long as God continues to give me life I WILL show you better than I can teach you and be the best role model I can be for you.

This book is dedicated solely to you. You were my motivation and inspiration when it came to writing this journal. As a young man, I enjoy watching you reach your milestones and enter into Manhood Bruh. Although it may be an awkward or confusing phase of life for you, I am here to guide you through it all even when we bump heads. Always remember I love you more than you know, even when you're irritable, emotional, defiant, and all those other emotions that come with puberty. Mommy ALWAYS gotcha Bru! 🤎

BRUH........ What the?

Hey Bruh,

My name is Maurice, and I am the youngest son of MsThomasRN. My mom is the author of #PERIODT which is a journal/ book about puberty for girls. She came to me and asked me if I wanted to help her in writing this "puberty book" for us guys. She asked me to write down my thoughts and ideas and promised me a co-author position in this book. I told her I'd give her my experience in exchange for all the answers to the questions I have because I know I'm not the only one going through this weird stage in my life BRUH! 🥴

I am 12 years old and a seventh grader in middle school 🫣. I am a Martial Artist and have enjoyed practicing self-defense (Jiu Jitsu) since I was three years old. I like to play sports and video games (my favorite game is Fortnite). When I'm not doing any of those hobbies, I enjoy robotics and building with my Legos (I am a master at Legos, I once built a character that was over 5,000 pieces… yeah BRUH!). When my mom lets me, I love showing off my skills in the kitchen as Chef Maurice. I'm not a pro just yet but I can cook up a little something. Sometimes I cook my mom breakfast, and she loves it too 😁. Now that you have an understanding of who I am, let's get to the real topic of this book.

My mom is a Registered Nurse, and she loves to help sick people, she's been doing this for a very long time. My mom also teaches boys and girls about their body parts, how they work and why it is important to know about your health. When I was seven years old my mom started to tell me about my body and continued to talk to me up until now. It was uncomfortable at first but now I can ask her anything without feeling ashamed or embarrassed. My mom and I just have that kinda relationship 😬.

About a year ago I noticed that EVERYTHING on my body was getting bigger. I knew I was going through puberty but WOA!....

I'll never forget this day BRUH. I was asleep and when I woke up in the morning, my underpants were wet. At first, I thought I peed on myself, but there wasn't a urine odor. When I got out of bed I went into the bathroom. I took off my underpants and saw that there were white stains on the front of them. This wet substance was sticky 🐵 ... Bruh, WHAT THE... 😬 !!! When I first experienced this I wasn't scared because my mom had told me about this and that it would happen. I went to my mom, and she sat me down to have a talk about my feelings of what happened. I was curious and she definitely had my attention BRUH! The first thing we spoke about was "that sticky white stuff" on my underpants and then she showed me some pictures. The pictures helped me to understand this a little more. I admit I was a little shy and made some silly faces because seeing a picture of a penis (other than mine) and these white "tadpole-like" things was weird. While my mom was talking to me about puberty I was horrified 😲 hearing this BRUH but I needed to know and so do you. I'm glad she had this conversation with me though. I'm not sure if you have a parent to talk to you about puberty but if you don't just keep reading. My mom made sure to put EVERYTHING you need to know about puberty in this book. Somethings are going to sound weird, and you may even feel uncomfortable but Dude... just take it all in, you need to know this so that you don't get caught off guard Bruh.

Maurice

Heeeey Handsome,

You are freaking amazing, and you are going to do amazing things with your life! This journal is just for you. It's a place for you to write down all of your personal thoughts and feelings while learning all about puberty.

Going through puberty is going to be rough if you haven't done so already. If you're going through puberty now, I'm sure you'll be able to relate to many things in this book. During this phase in your life, you are going to be overwhelmed with so much information 📕 about the changes happening in your body. Your friends will talk to you, you'll get information from social media sites, television and/or the internet that may not all be true. The reason I wrote this journal for you is because I want you to get the most up to date and accurate information about puberty from me. I've been a nurse in this field for a very long time, and I've seen and done just about everything you can imagine. I am NO stranger to men's health, so I wanted to share what I know in my years as a reproductive nurse with you.

First things first, you CAN NOT escape puberty BRUH😎! It is normal and it is a part of your life as you transition to manhood. Talking about puberty, believe it or not will relieve a lot of anxiety when these changes start happening to you. I want you to be prepared before these changes even happen and comfortable when they do happen so that you are not scared, confused and /or surprised when your body starts to change.

Some of the topics in this journal may be weird, awkward or even uncomfortable as you read them but, I hope that you are receptive to this information and embrace it. If you have a dad or guardian you can talk to about puberty, I encourage you to do so. I know you may want to talk to your friends especially if they're going through puberty as well, but remember puberty is different for everyone. His symptoms may not be the same as yours so please don't rely on "his" experiences to be "your" experiences.

It is very important for you to know about your body and why it is so vital to your reproductive health, so let's talk about it, BRUH😎

Children's Rights

The Right to be children.
The Right to have fun.
The Right to have feelings and ideas and to express them.
The Right to ask for what they need.
The Right to some secrets.
The Right to say no.
The Right to Privacy.
The Right to make certain choices.
The Right to feel safe.
The Right to be respected.
The Right to be accepted for who they are.
The Right to know their limits.
The Right to be nurtured and cared for.
The Right to a support system, including peers.
and supportive adults.
The Rights to rewards and natural consequences.
The Right to be protected from abuse or neglect.
The Right to be believed.
The Right to a relationship with their parents.
The Right to be protected from knowledge beyond their years.
The Right not to worry about grown-up problems.
The Right to be HAPPY

(author Unknown)

Table of Contents

Hey, handsome, it's me, Nurse Monica. Let's talk so I can tell you some interesting things about yourself. How well do you know yourself inside and out? Let me take you on a trip. A trip filled with everything that has to do with you and what's going on in that body of yours. I'm here to give you some business, get all in your business and force you to get to know yourself better than you already do. Can I do that? I want you to think about some serious things and I hope that all the questions you have will be answered and clear to you after reading this journal. Let's jump right into things.

What do you already know about your body? 🤯

_____

_____

_____

_____

_____

What would you like to know about your body? 🤯

_____

_____

_____

_____

_____

Tell me a little about yourself. 😬

_____

_____

_____

_____

_____

_____

_____

_____

Wow! You're a really cool dude 😎, BRUH! Thank you for sharing a little about yourself with me.

"Y" am I a #Male

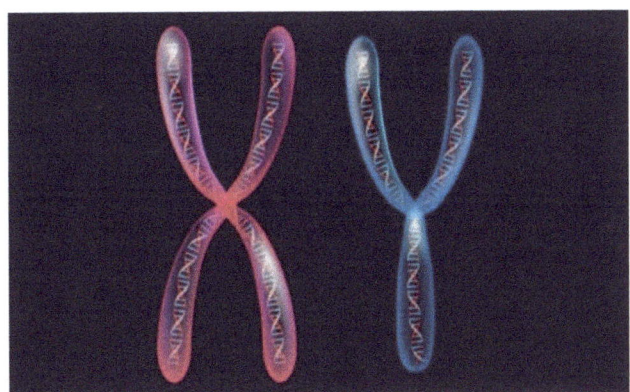

The Y chromosome is ONLY present in males. Simply put it is responsible for you being a male. You are born with a YX which makes you a male. The X chromosome is ONLY present in females and therefore is responsible for the making of a female, XX makes her a female.

What is a chromosome?

Chromosomes are chemical instructions that tell your body how to grow and develop. They make up who you will become. Half of these instructions came from your dad, and the other half came from your mom when your mom was pregnant with you. You are who you are and what you look like because of these chromosomes. So, thank your parents for the handsome guy you are becoming.

#Testosterone

The Male Hormone

Pronounced (tes-TOS-teh-rone), testosterone is the hormone (chemicals in your body that sends messages to organs in your body and tells them what to do) in your body that is responsible for some of the changes you will go through during puberty. Testosterone is made in your testes (balls) and helps in the development of your reproductive organs, growing body hair, muscle strength, deep voice, sperm and other changes in your body.

Testosterone is produced in men and women but is considered the "male hormone" because it is more abundant in men. Look at the picture below and all the effects testosterone has on your body. What do you think?

_____

_____

_____

_____

_____

_____

_____

The EFFECTS of TESTOSTERONE

BONES
Bone mass
density maintenance

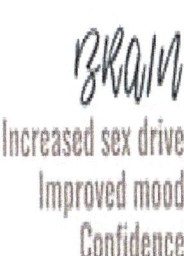 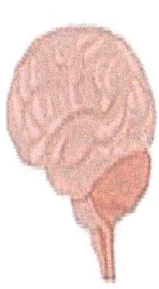

BRAIN
Increased sex drive
Improved mood
Confidence
Memory function

MUSCLES
Muscle growth
Increased strength
Increased endurance

BONE MARROW
Red blood cell
production

SKIN
Hair growth
Collagen growth

 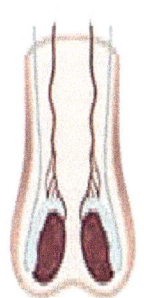

SEX ORGANS
Sperm production
Eriktile function
Prostate growth

genesysmenshealth.com

3

#MyManParts

Male Reproductive System

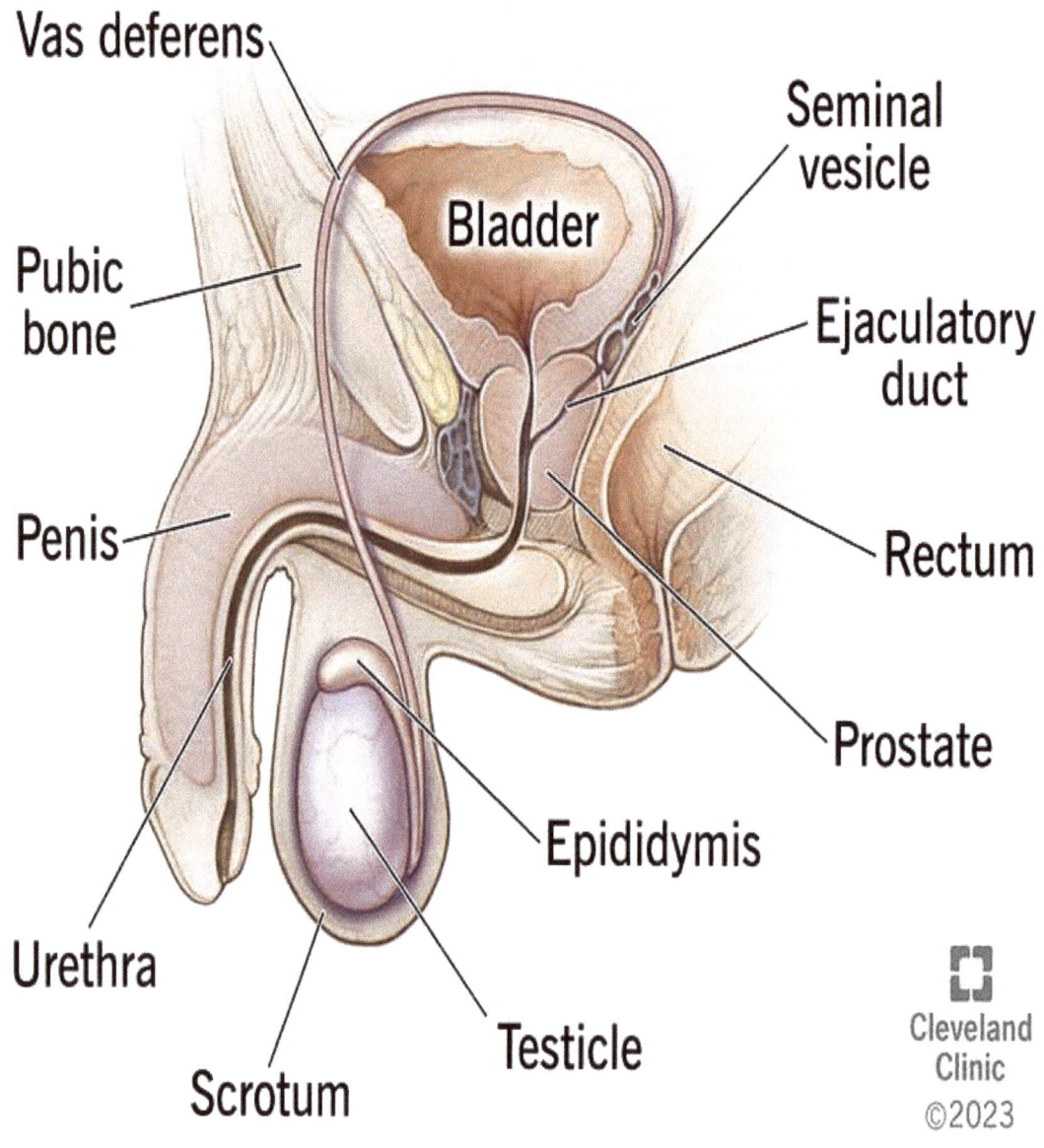

Tell me what you think your reproductive system is?

_____

_____

_____

_____

_____

_____

Tell me why you think it is important?

_____

_____

_____

_____

_____

_____

Your reproductive system consists of internal (inside) and external (outside) organs inside of your body? What is an organ, you may ask? According to Merriam- Webster, an organ is a group of different tissues that work together to perform a specific function in your body. For example, your muscles and your bones work together so that it is possible for you to move. The main purpose of your reproductive system is to produce the hormone (Testosterone, which is released from your brain) which works together with your other reproductive organs (penis and testicles). When these organs work together they make it possible for you to get a female pregnant so that she can have a baby, of course when you're older and mature.

I just mentioned two of your main reproductive organs (penis and testicles) but there are so many more. Let's talk about them and find out what exactly they do. The diagram below is a picture of what these organs look like.

Now that you know what your reproductive organs look like, let's explain their importance and functions. If you notice some of your organs hang outside of your body while the others are inside. Let's test your knowledge really quick:

Which organs can you see and feel outside of your body?

_____

_____

_____

_____

_____

_____

_____

Which organs can't you see 👀 because they are inside of your body?

_____

_____

_____

_____

_____

_____

_____

MY OUTSIDE REPRODUCTIVE ORGANS

#PENIS-   Your penis hangs outside of your body. It is shaped like a long tube. The purpose of your penis is to bring semen, sperm and urine outside of your body. It has three parts to it.

1. The ROOT of your penis is attached to the wall of your abdomen.

2. The SHAFT of your penis is also known as the body of your penis. It is stretchy, very sensitive and comes in all sizes. As you go through puberty, you will notice that it grows larger. You may also notice that it gets really stiff at times (erection). An erection happens when your penis gets really hard, it gets larger, longer and "stands up away from your body" (erect) because lots of blood flows to this area. This usually happens when you are excited and/ or aroused (to be stimulated by sights, sounds, thoughts, or physical touch).

3. The GLANS of your penis is also known as the head. It is also known as the "extra skin" (foreskin) if you are not circumcised. If you are circumcised (I'll explain circumcision later on) it looks like the ice cream 🍦 inside of a cone.....lol😂.

#FORESKIN-
Your foreskin, is a flap of skin that protects and covers the head/glans of your penis. When you are born some parents have this skin removed, this is called circumcision, and I'll tell you more about that soon.

#SCROTUM-
Your scrotum hangs outside of your body and is located behind your penis. It kind of looks like a wrinkled pouch sac. The purpose of your scrotum is to hold 2 small egg shaped organs known as your testicles aka testes. This pouch protects your testicles and keeps them warm. If you didn't know, your scrotum has muscles in them, yes muscles. These muscles help your scrotum to get tight and also to relax. When it tightens, your testicles move closer to your body, this keeps them warm and protected. When the scrotum relaxes, your testicles move away from your body and cools down. Imagine that your scrotum operates like a stove and a refrigerator...... lol 🤣

#TESTICLES-
Most boys are born with two testicles inside the scrotum. If you ever wondered what they look like, your testicles look like two boiled eggs 🥚 🥚 ... lol. Their job is to produce sperm and testosterone. In order for this to happen your testicles must be kept at a certain temperature. Your scrotum helps to protect and regulate this temperature of your testes.

As you can see, the penis, the scrotum, and the testes are located outside of your body. If you look at the picture below, you will see how they all look. Does this look familiar to you?

Testicles

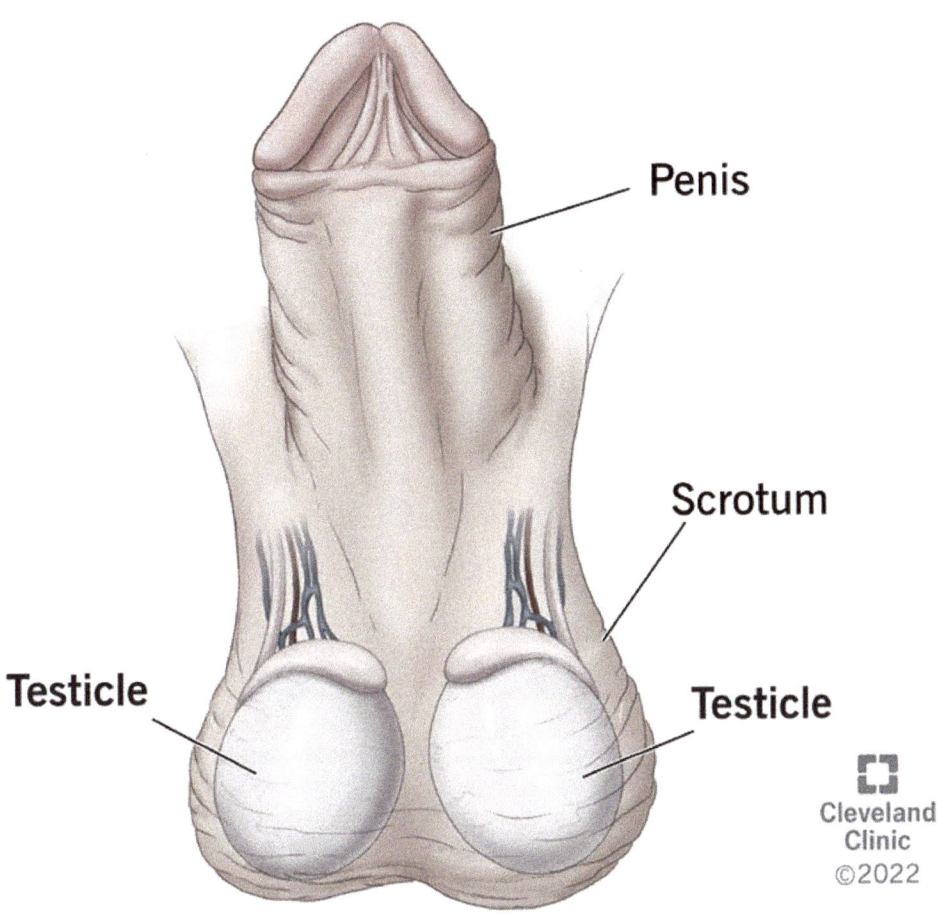

Penis

Scrotum

Testicle

Testicle

Cleveland
Clinic
©2022

#Circumcision

To Be or Not To Be!

If you were determined to be a boy while your mother was pregnant with you, you were more than likely born with a penis. All baby boys are born with skin that covers the end of their penis. This skin is called "foreskin" and is known as an "uncircumcised penis". Some parents decide to have this skin removed (cut off) when you are born😫. Now this may sound really painful and will be, especially if you were to have this done now at your age. This is why it is done days after a baby boy is born. This procedure involves a medical provider cutting off the skin that covers your penis and is known as "circumcision".

Why is Circumcision done? Circumcision is very common and there are a few reasons why parents choose to have their baby boys circumcised. One reason is due to religion. In some religions circumcision symbolizes purification and a contract with God. Another reason for circumcision is for hygiene reasons. According to Kids Health, 2022, removing the foreskin on the penis makes it easier to clean when you are a baby and reduces urinary tract infections. When you become older and sexually active circumcision reduces sexually transmitted infections and cancer.

Now if your parents choose not to have you circumcised that is not a bad thing. Your risk of having more infections is greater, so hygiene will be very important for you.

It is important to bathe daily as you go through puberty and to pull the foreskin of your penis back to clean it well with soap and water. This prevents bacteria from building up under the extra skin and prevents infection. If you are not circumcised your penis will look like the penis on the left. If you are circumcised your penis will look like the penis on the left. Whether or not you're circumcised, your penis serves the same purpose.

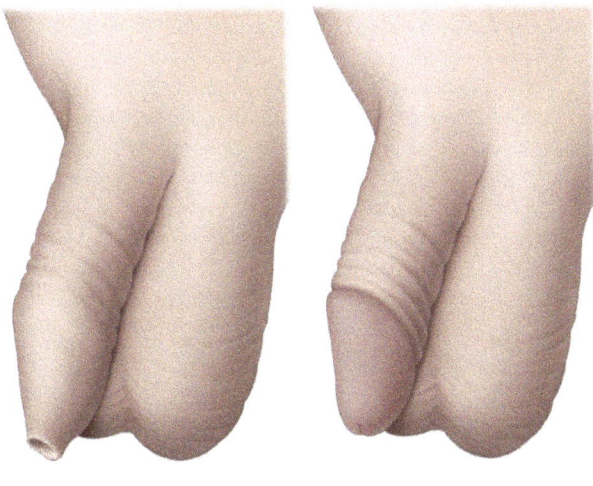

Your Thoughts 🤔

_____

_____

_____

_____

_____

_____

_____

MY INTERNAL
REPRODUCTIVE ORGANS

Male Reproductive System

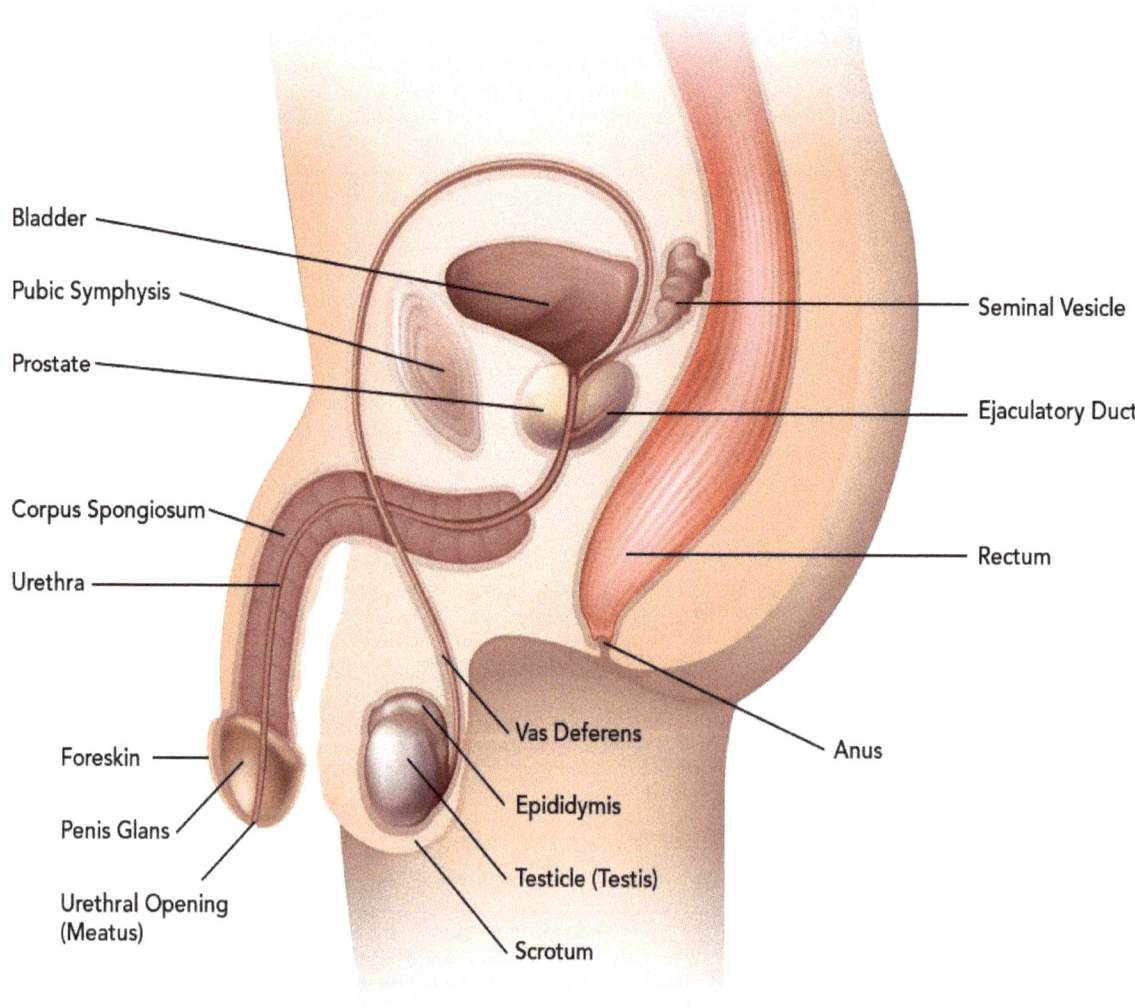

Bladder

Pubic Symphysis

Prostate

Corpus Spongiosum

Urethra

Foreskin

Penis Glans

Urethral Opening
(Meatus)

Seminal Vesicle

Ejaculatory Duct

Rectum

Vas Deferens

Anus

Epididymis

Testicle (Testis)

Scrotum

https://ygeiax.com/pages/male-reproductive-system

#Urethra-

What is your urethra? Well, let me explain it like this. In the center of the head of your penis there is an opening. This opening is the end of a long tube that is connected to your bladder (look at the picture of your reproductive organs). Find the beginning of your urethral opening in your penis and take your finger and follow it to your bladder. The purpose of your urethra is to allow urine (pee) and semen (we'll discuss this later) to come out of your penis.

#Epididymis-

Look at the picture of your organs and locate your epididymis. It sits on top of both of your testicles. The sperm in your testicles is immature but when sperm goes to your epididymis it gets stored here where your sperm then matures so they are ready for fertilization.

#Vas Deferens-

Your Vas Deferens is the long tube that you see in the picture of your reproductive organs. I'll give you a minute to locate and trace it with your finger. As you can see it starts in your epididymis (in your scrotum) and it joins the seminal vesicle. After they join together the tube continues and becomes your urethra.

The purpose of your vas deferens is to carry the mature sperm cells and semen from your epididymis to your penis where it exits your urethra opening.

#Seminal Vesicle-

Look at the picture of your reproductive organs and locate your seminal vesicle, I'll give you a minute. Your seminal vesicles look like a small tornado in this picture...lol. If you look closely it is connected to your vas deferens and behind your bladder. You're probably asking yourself, What the?......What is this and what does it do? Well let's discuss it. This organ is responsible for providing your sperm with the energy it needs to move around and swim really fast. Think of it as the gas station of your reproductive organs. The "gas" is the fluid aka (ejaculatory fluid) added with "sugar" to give your sperm energy.

#Prostate Gland– Before I explain what your prostate gland is let me

explain what a "gland" is. A gland is an organ in your body that performs a certain function in your body. Their job is to produce fluids, for example sweat and saliva (spit). In this case your prostate gland helps to produce fluid as well. Locate your prostate gland in the picture. It looks like a small rock and is about the size of a strawberry in this picture. At this time your prostate is a little smaller than a strawberry but as you grow it will grow. It's located right underneath your bladder. The fluid from your prostate gland joins the fluid from your seminal vesicle and together they form semen.

#Semen– Tell me what you think Semen is?

_____

_____

_____

Semen is a fluid in your body that is produced by your "glands". Semen is only made by men. This fluid is whitish in color, and it is "sticky" (that's what I have been told... 😂 lol). This fluid comes out of your penis during an orgasm (I'll explain this to you later on). Semen contains fluid from the seminal vesicle and your prostate. Together they come together to help "sperm" travel through your reproductive organs and out of your body. This fluid is deposited into a female (during sex) and helps to create a baby that will grow inside of her body. I will also tell you more about this later on.

#The Ejaculatory Duct- Your ejaculatory duct is a small tunnel

that helps carry sperm and semen out of your urethra during an ejaculation. Take a look at it in the picture.

#SpermCells- You were born Male. Only males produce sperm cells that

make it necessary for you to reproduce (have children). When you were born you did not produce sperm but sperm production starts when you begin puberty. It's very similar to a girl getting her period. In order for boys and girls to reproduce their reproductive organs must mature and produce sperm (male) and eggs (female) to make that happen. When you begin puberty you will begin to produce sperm inside of your testicles. These sperm cells are immature (not ready to produce a baby). Your epididymitis then takes those immature sperm cells and stores them until they are mature enough and ready to make a baby. Do you understand that? _____. One sperm cell is 10x smaller than a grain of salt (that's REALLY small). During an ejaculation (I'll explain this in a moment) you'll release millions of sperm cells that are mixed in semen. Each sperm cell has a head, a neck (middle) and a tail which helps it swim. They kinda resemble a tadpole. Take a look at this picture of a single sperm cell.

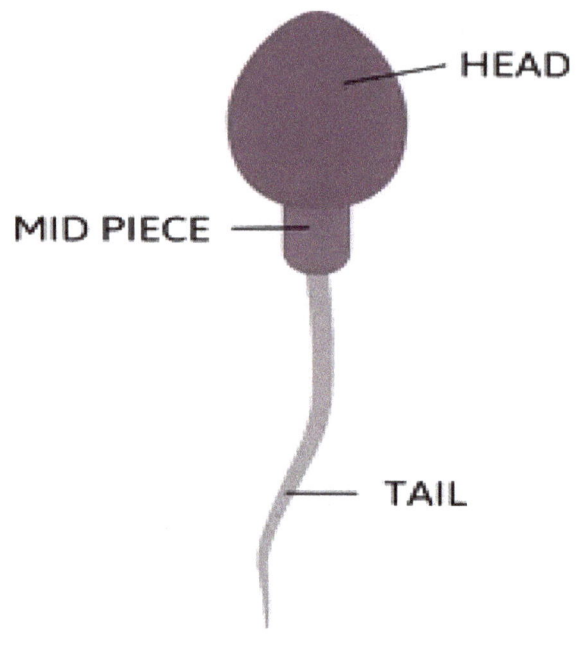

HEAD

MID PIECE

TAIL

As you go through puberty those sperm cells will eventually mature and when they come out of your body and are placed inside of the female's body, they can make a baby. Now you may want to know, how do these sperm cells get out of your body? Let's talk about that.

But first let me give you a fun fact about your sperm. When you start to produce sperm, your body will make millions and millions of sperm for the rest of your life BUT..... It only takes ONE sperm to fertilize the female's egg. Imagine if you had a dollar for every sperm you produced....... You'd be a millionaire 🤑 BRUH!

BRUH, let's stop for a minute and put this all together. The purpose of your reproductive system is to work together so that your organs can produce sperm that make it possible for you to have children in the future. This process starts in your testicles and ends with the ejaculation of sperm from your penis.

Think about all that you've read so far. What's your thoughts? 🫢

_____

_____

_____

_____

_____

_____

_____

Male Reproductive Crossword

```
N U R E T H R A W Y O W S C S A B
R L O P Q C J E B F P B C M G J V
L D B D S O J P L Q H P R E L C A
L U A Y G L S I Q P H R O R L R S
X A N U S O C D T J S O T E K Q D
I Z B H A N Y Y E B V S U C O L E
Z Q N Q F O W D S O E T M T C S F
V R E C T U M I T C L A Y I P G E
T P E N I S K M I T M T I L U O R
Y G Q R B P B I C H A E W E B A E
T H K W L E L S L H L S S T I V N
Y Q Q D A V I C E L I S D I C E S
K E O J D S C O S V K Y A S B S F
I T W U D K A M T L E H C S O Y M
K S O M E L D X Q Z C Y K U N P P
R F D O R Z X W Z D J E Z E E Q N
O M E J A C U L A T O R Y D U C T
```

Ejaculatory duct	Erectile tissue	Vas deferens
Pubic bone	Epidydimis	Testicles
Prostate	Scrotum	Bladder
Urethra	Rectum	Colon
Penis	Anus	

#StickyTopics

#Ejaculation-Cum On Bruh

While explaining the functions of your reproductive system I mentioned the word ejaculation. I would like to explain to you what exactly that is. To begin, ejaculation is a part of your puberty stage, and it includes the production of sperm. Your reproductive organs work together to release sperm cells and semen (cum) from your penis. This usually happens when you are aroused (excited in a pleasurable way). When this happens, your penis becomes erect (hard) and your muscles contract. Your muscle along with these contractions force sperm and semen to exit your penis. This is known as an ejaculation. Have you had this experience?

_____

_____

_____

_____

_____

_____

#Erection-
Now that you are going through puberty, you may have noticed that your penis gets really hard and may "stand straight up". This is called an erection Bruh. This happens when you become aroused (excited). You may notice that this happens a lot at night time (during a wet dream) or when you wake up and stretch in the morning. During an erection the penis becomes stiff and gets slightly larger because tissue surrounding the penis fills up with blood. This can be very uncomfortable for you. Have you had this happen to you and if so how do you feel about this?

_____

_____

_____

#Wet Dreams-
What is a wet dream? During puberty you may have several wet dreams. A wet dream usually happens at night time while you're dreaming. The dream is usually a sexual dream that makes you excited. Your penis becomes erect, and this erection leads to semen coming from your penis. When you wake up you may notice that your underwear are wet and there's a "sticky" fluid around your private area. This is a normal part of puberty, and it may make you uncomfortable in the beginning. As you become older it may happen more often, you're becoming a man BRUH, and this is all normal.

#Blue Balls -
Blue balls is a term used to describe the discomfort of your scrotum. This happens when you get an erection BUT do not ejaculate or have an orgasm. Due to the blood that rushes to the penis and the scrotum during the erection, your scrotum turns a bluish or purplish color for a few moments. I've been told that it is very uncomfortable and at times can be very painful. I did some research and I found that distracting yourself by thinking of something else can cause your penis to return to its "flaccid" (limp, not erect) state.

#Orgasm -
An orgasm is a pleasurable feeling you get in your penis, it's sought of like a sneeze. Just like mucus may come out of your nose when you sneeze, semen and sperm come out of your penis (aka ejaculation). Initially you may not have sex, but this pleasurable feeling may happen if you masturbate. Masturbation is when you touch/stimulate yourself (usually your penis) to make yourself feel good. This is normal behavior especially while you're going through puberty.

_____

_____

_____

_____

_____

_____

_____

Your Urinary System

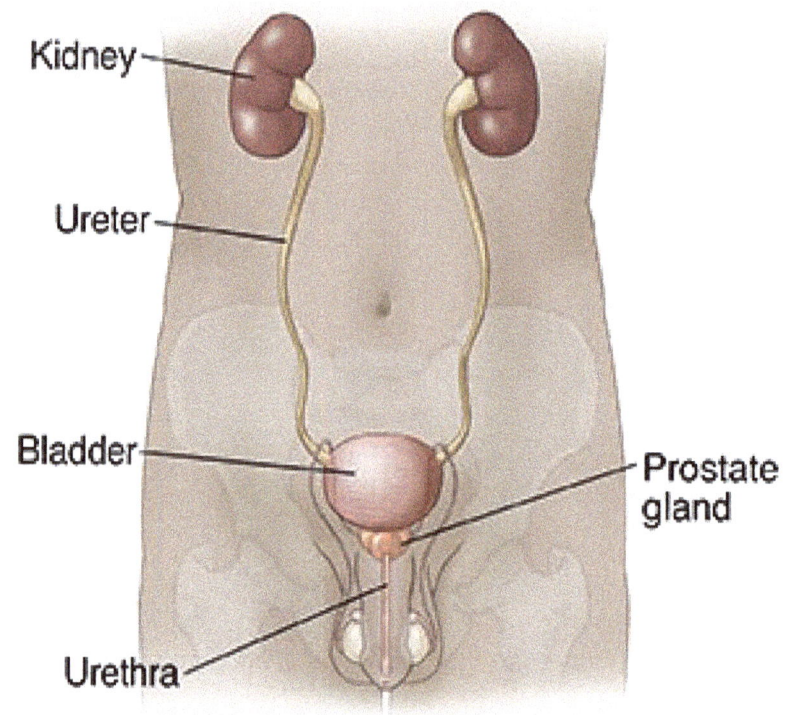

Your urinary system is not a part of your reproductive system but because both these systems depend on each other to work, it is important that I provide this information to you as well. The purpose of this system is to get rid of your body's waste (urine).

#Kidneys- Look at the picture of your urinary system and locate your

kidneys. Would you agree that they look like kidney beans? Well, your kidneys filter (cleans) your blood. They gather up all of the toxins and water your body doesn't need and get rid of it by making urine.

#Ureters- After your kidneys filter urine, it travels down your uterus (2 tubes which are connected to your kidneys) down to your bladder. This is their only purpose.

#BLADDER- Your bladder is not officially a part of your reproductive system; it is a part of your urinary system. It is a strong muscle about the size of your fist. It is able to stretch and contract like a balloon. Its main function is to hold your urine (pee) and empty it through a tube (urethra) that is located in your penis. When it fills up, your brain sends a signal to let you know that you have to let the urine out.

#Urethra- This is a tube that carries urine from your bladder out of the body through your penis. If you remember your urethra also brings sperm and semen out of your penis but this CAN NOT happen at the same time. Your Thoughts: 😳

_____

_____

_____

_____

_____

Your rectum and your anus are located near your reproductive organs and are a part of your digestive system (this system starts in your mouth. The food you eat travels down your body, is broken down and used to feed your organs, what's not used (poop) exits your body through your anus).

#Rectum-

Your rectum is like a holding cell for your stool (poop) until you are ready to expel it from your body. If you look at the picture of your reproductive organs, you will see what it looks like.

#Anus-

Your anus is attached to your rectum. It is the opening through which stool (poop) leaves your body.

Now that you know about your body parts, let's talk about how they all work during puberty. But first, what do you think about what you just read? 🧐

_____

_____

_____

_____

_____

#Puberty

Becoming a Man

_____

_____

_____

_____

Technically speaking, puberty is nature's way of transforming your body from a boy child to an adult man so that you can reproduce (being able to have children) in the future. It's a process but it doesn't happen all at once and it doesn't happen to everyone at the same time. Puberty happens sometime between 9-18 years old. Your body will change in new and exciting ways and most times it can and will be confusing and/or awkward for you. Not only does your body change physically, so do your emotions and the decisions you will make. The friends you hang out with or the hobbies or activities you choose may also change. You are growing up and that is Ok Bruh!

So, what's causing all of these changes? Hormones! Hormones! Hormones! This change is possible due to hormones in your body. What are hormones you may ask? According to the CDC, hormones are chemical messengers in your body that regulate many bodily functions and are important for life and health. For example, as you go through puberty, you may notice that your penis and/or your muscles are beginning to grow larger. This is due to hormonal changes in your body. The hormone responsible for triggering all these changes in your body is called Testosterone and it is known as the Male Hormone.

During puberty, you may notice lots of changes happening to you. Let's look at some of the physical changes you can expect to see. Circle the changes you are going through or have gone through already. Then let's talk about them.

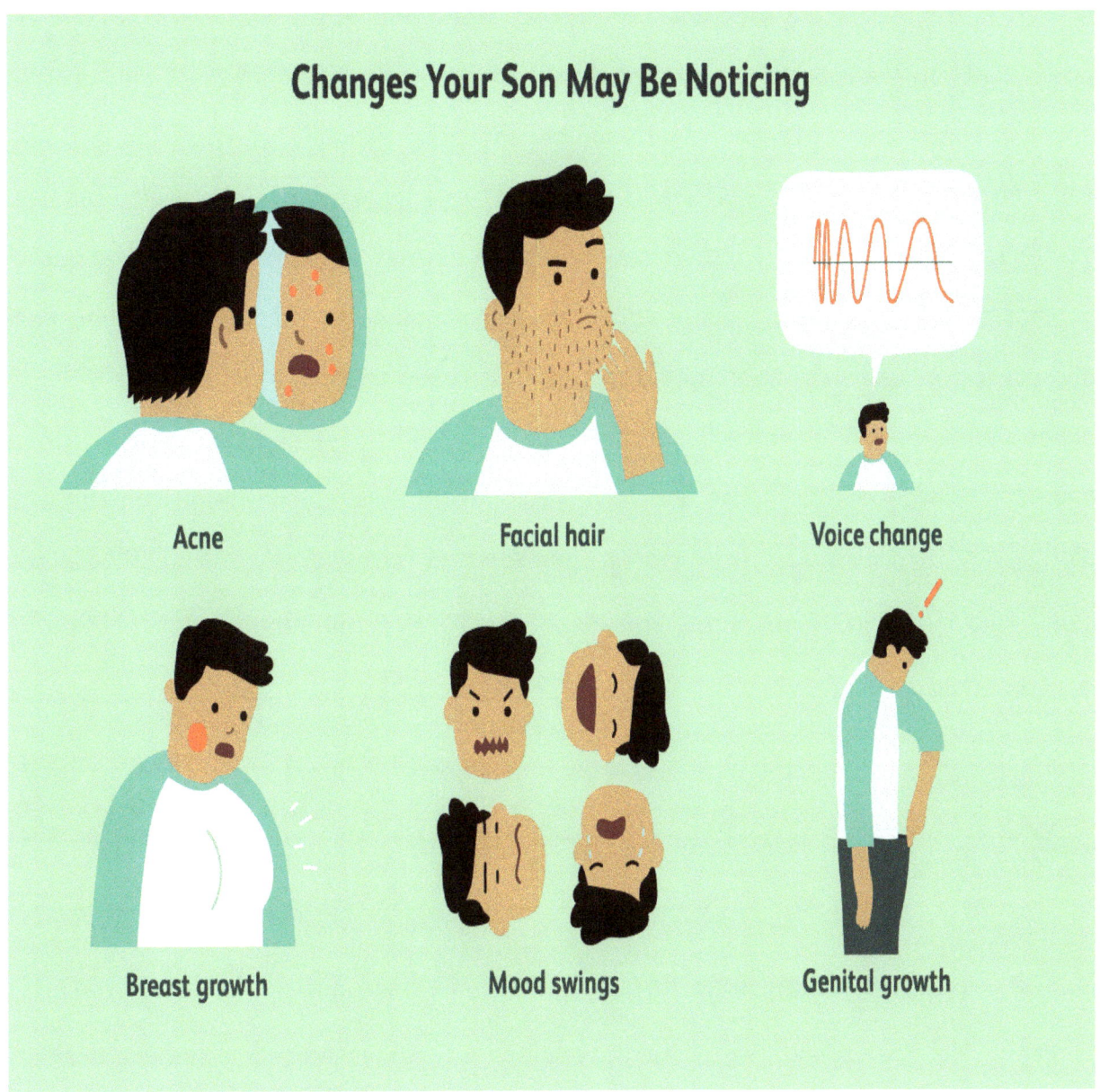

parents.com

Growth spurt: During puberty you may feel like you're growing taller very fast. Your hands, your feet, your penis and your muscles are also getting larger. This is normal and all a part of puberty, you're literally "Growing Up Bruh". Because you are growing so fast, you may notice your body is achy and this is because your bones and muscles are stretching. You may find that you are more tired and sleepy, and this is all due to you growing so fast. Rest often but don't sleep your life away Bruh. You may also be hungrier and find yourself eating everything in the refrigerator. Water, fruits and healthy foods are a better choice for your appetite, IJS… 😐. This growth spurt is sometimes determined by your parents. For example, if your dad is really tall, you may be tall and even taller than him. If your parents are short, you will still go through a growth spurt, but it may not seem as fast as others. Don't feel bad if you notice your friends are taller than you, you are all going through these changes, and you'll eventually catch up with them. By the time you're in your mid-teens, you'll probably be the height you will be for the rest of your life. Here's a cool idea: stand against the wall in your house and have your parents mark your height on the wall along with the date every three months and see how fast you're growing. (Please get your parents' permission before you start marking up their walls…. Lol 😳

_____

_____

_____

_____

Voice changes: As you go through puberty you will notice that your voice is changing. You may sound like a squeaky duck or a croaking frog 🐸. This is a normal part of your development, and it is temporary. It definitely sounds weird but guess what, you are not alone, most boys go through this and every boy goes through it at different times. So, what is causing this sound? Well, inside of your throat there is a tube that is very stretchy like a rubber band called your larynx or your voice box.

When air hits these tubes they vibrate and this allows you to speak, sing, yell and create sound (voice). As your body grows during puberty, the larynx grows too. As the tube grows bigger your voice sounds will change and become deeper causing your voice to crack, squeal or croak 🐸 .

Have you noticed a change in your voice? If so, how do you feel about this? 🫣

_____

_____

_____

_____

_____

_____

_____

_____

Body hair: Due to a rise in testosterone your body will start to grow more hair. Boys usually grow more hair than girls. Hair is important because it helps to protect your skin and keep your body temperature cool. Hair will become more visible on your face, under the arms, your legs and even around your penis. The first place you may notice hair is around your penis. Take a look at this picture.

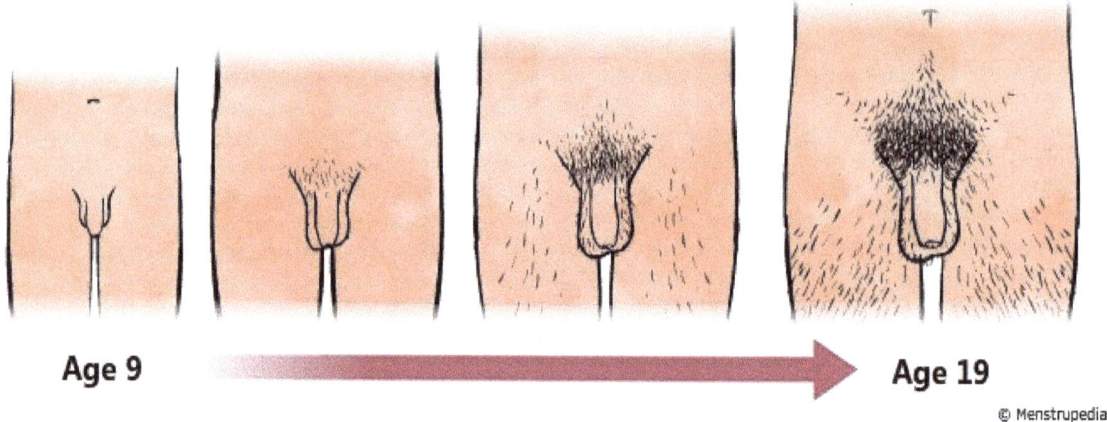

Age 9 → Age 19

© Menstrupedia

Facial hair will start to grow soon after you notice hair around your penis. It usually starts above your lips. This is called a mustache. Most boys are really happy about this facial hair because it says, I'm becoming a man, I'm confident and I'm handsome.

Underarm hair is another place you'll notice hair growth. Guys usually let the hair under their arms grow; they don't cut it. Whatever you decide is your choice though. If your hair grows really fast under your armpit be sure to wash it daily so that it does not have an odor. Remember sweat and bacteria live on your hair too.

Hair on your legs and arms will grow as well. Most guys don't shave their legs but again this is your choice.

Genital changes: During puberty your scrotum and your testicals become larger and may get darker, this is normal. Your penis is made up of blood and stretchy skin that expands just like a balloon. Your genitals are very delicate and very sensitive so be careful not to hurt yourself Bruh! It is important to know that your penis does NOT have any bones. It may seem like it especially when you have an erection (stiff penis) but it doesn't 😶.

Due to an increase in size, you may even start having erections and ejaculations more often.

How do you feel about these changes?

_____

_____

_____

_____

Body Appearance: You will notice a change in the build of your body. For example, your muscles may become larger (you may find yourself flexing in the mirror 💪 ...lol) and you may also feel stronger (don't hurt anybody Bruh!). You are changing into a handsome young man. It may feel weird, but you'll start to embrace this change afterwhile.

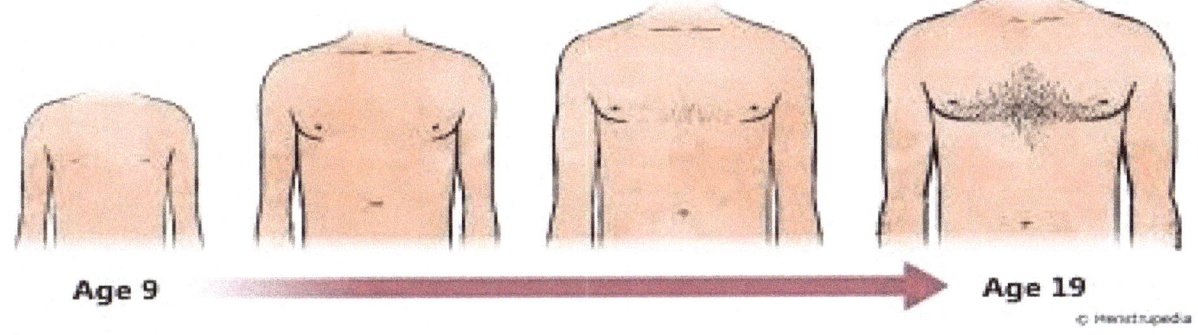

Age 9 ————————————————————➤ Age 19
© Menstrupedia

Skin changes: Due to your hormones, your skin may become oily. This may cause acne (pimples and /or blackheads). Acne can be a pain in the butt, but it's a part of puberty and it can be very overwhelming for some guys. Shower daily to prevent a buildup of oil and bacteria (the cause of acne) on your skin and especially your face.

One piece of advice I'd like to give you is…. DO NOT POP PIMPLES, especially on your face 😁. This can leave a scar that looks worse than the pimple before you popped it. Eventually it will go away on its own, just try to keep your face as clean as possible. If acne becomes really bad talk to your mom or a health care provider for treatment. Some medicines help prevent or reduce acne and they can be purchased at a pharmacy.

Having acne can cause you to feel ugly, embarrassed or have low self-esteem. This can lead to being bullied and make you feel bad about yourself when you're around other people. Unfortunately, you may not be able to control acne all the time but practice good hygiene, eat well and ignore the rude comments Bruh.

_____

_____

_____

_____

_____

_____

_____

_____

_____

#Hygiene

What is Body Odor Bruh?

So, you are going through puberty and you're not alone. I'm sure your friends are experiencing similar changes in their bodies as well. During puberty your parents may tell you to shower/ bathe more often. Why do you think that is 😯?

_____

_____

_____

Now that your body is going through changes, you may notice that your body odor is also changing. You are sweating (perspiration) more often, and your body odor is on high alert (like your armpits) .... DUDE, why is that 😖? Well to begin with, your body is covered with lots of good bacteria (very tiny living organisms that live all over your body and even in your mouth). This bacteria doesn't bother you at all, it's just there chilling. Your body also contains a mixture of salt and water. Here are 2 simple equations:

1. Body salt + water + bacteria = Smelly body odor 🤢

2. Body odor + shower with soap and water = a good smelling body 🤗.

You may notice this smell if you haven't showered in a while... 🤢 Really Bruh! That's not cool. Smelly body odor can cause people to make fun of you and even bully you and I know you don't want that. If you play sports, more than likely you will sweat, and some guys will sweat more than others. After playing sports it's ALWAYS a good idea to shower afterwards to prevent you from having bad body odor. Showering daily (personal hygiene) is the BEST way to prevent a smelly body and it is good practice to keep your body neat and clean. If you're not able to shower daily make sure to clean under your armpits and between your legs (groin area) and your feet with soap and water. These areas are important because in these areas you have extra skin that folds. More bacteria and sweat will go to these areas, get trapped and stay there until they are washed away. If it's not washed the sweat and bacteria will start smelling really bad. Good hygiene is more than just washing your body with soap and water. What about your hair? What about your mouth? Those areas need daily cleaning too, let's talk about it Bruh!

Here are a few hygiene pointers:

- Make sure to wash the hair on your head because hair can also carry bacteria and sweat. If you don't wash it often it will start to smell. If you wear braids, it's a good idea to redo them often. Hair oils and gels start to smell after a while. If you can't get your hair rebraided, wash your hair with the braids in it, this will at least cut down on the smell. Haircuts are cool too, just make sure to wash your hair often especially if you use hair care products. If you wear a dude rag, wash it weekly so that it does not smell. Remember your head sweats too and your hair carries bacteria and moisture. This is a recipe for a smelly dude rag 🤢.

- Brushing your teeth should be done when you wake up, before you go to bed and preferably after any meal. If you can't do that make sure to brush your teeth before you go to bed. If food is left in your mouth overnight, this can cause plaque and/or tooth decay and a smelly mouth in the morning. Brush for 4-5 minutes and don't forget to use Listerine (mouth wash} to get rid of those smelly germs you could not reach with the brush. Bad breath is not cool Bruh, and the girls will not like it or talk to you 🤢.

- Make sure to put on deodorant after you bathe. Deodorant and antiperspirants help prevent sweat and smelly armpits. If you don't use deodorant because of your religion or culture, make sure to wash under your arms really well and daily to prevent a smelly armpit. Fella's, these products ONLY WORK on a CLEAN armpit! 🧼 Please DO NOT put deodorant on a smelly armpit, you will STILL smell… 😱. You must wash the bacteria and sweat off first, if not it won't work. If you can't shower daily, clean under your armpits with soap and water and then apply deodorant, it works much better, trust me Bruh!

- You may notice that your feet smell really bad when you take your shoes off 🤢. This is because your feet sweat more than any other part of your body. This sweat has bacteria that loves to live in warm, moist places (the inside of your shoe). It's almost as if the bacteria have invited all of their friends (sweat, fungus and more bacteria) to a party in your sneakers… LOL 🤣. When ALL of them get together, they become trapped in your sneakers and can't get out until you take your shoes off. To prevent smelly feet, shower and wash them daily. Make sure to clean in between EVERY toe. Use a toothbrush (not the one you use for your teeth) to brush in between your toenails. Cut or file your toenails if they are too long, this will also help cut back on the smell. Put on clean socks EVERYDAY. It does not make sense to put a smelly sock back on a clean foot, that's just weird Bruh 😖. If you don't have clean socks daily, wash your socks out every day so that they will be clean and fresh for the next day. Wearing the same sneaker also contributes to smelly feet. Now I know not everyone has more than one pair of sneakers and that's ok, no judgement here. However, take your shoes off as soon as you get home and you can use disinfectant spray to kill the bacteria and sweat germs in your shoes daily. This will reduce the odor in your shoes.

- Cleaning the inside of your ears is also a part of your personal hygiene. This can easily be done while you're in the shower. Ear wax is a normal part of your body development and is not a bad thing. But since we are talking about hygiene, it's a good idea to clean them often to prevent buildup of earwax. This does not need to be done every single day but at least 1-2 times a week. Using a special ear Q-Tip can prevent you from putting the Q-Tip too far down in your ear. Ask your parents to buy a few the next time they go grocery shopping.

- Make sure to clean yourself well when you poop Bruh. Everyone poops 💩, it's nothing to be embarrassed about. Use as much toilet paper as you need to clean up back there. A smelly butt and /or stained underpants is definitely embarrassing especially if mom is washing your clothes…. I'm just saying 🙄.

- The last part of keeping up with your hygiene is washing your hands and keeping your nails short and clean. I believe good hand washing is probably the most important part of your hygiene. Think about this 🤔, your hands touch EVERYTHING and EVERYTHING has germs (bacteria) on it. It is very easy to transfer the germs on your hands to your body (mainly your face) just by touching it. The germs are so small that you don't even see them. For example, when you go to school, you touch the doorknob to open the door, right? Well, if someone touched it before you did and they had a cold germ, it's possible that that germ is now on the doorknob. You come behind them and touch the doorknob and then you touch your face, it's possible that you just rubbed their germs onto your face and now you will be sick too 🤧 . So how do you prevent something like this from happening?

- 1. Carry hand sanitizer in your bag. You may not be able to wash your hands all the time, but you can limit the amount of germs on your hands by using this. The alcohol that's in hand sanitizer will help to kill the bacteria from the "things" you have touched and prevent the spread of germs.

- 2. Washing your hands with soap and water will always be the best way to prevent the spread of germs. It's a good idea to always clean your hands before you eat, when you enter your home and several times when you're outside of your home. Good hand washing is the best way to defend your body Bruh!

Your thoughts about hygiene: 🤔

_____

_____

_____

_____

_____

PERSONAL HYGIENE
WORD SEARCH

Solve the following puzzle by finding all the hidden words!

BATH

TOWEL

FLOSS

WASH

SOAP

HYGIENE

GERMS

ROUTINE

SHOWER

COMB

CLEAN

MOUTHWASH

NAIL CLIPPER

SHAMPOO

TOILET PAPER

E	M	T	A	T	I	B	C	E	G	A	T	C	N	P	R	N
N	H	Y	G	I	E	N	E	E	A	I	B	P	S	B	A	P
I	T	O	O	T	H	B	R	U	S	H	T	T	T	I	B	L
T	T	E	I	S	W	M	O	S	S	G	O	M	L	T	T	U
U	H	R	O	H	S	N	U	T	C	L	I	C	T	P	T	N
O	S	E	E	A	W	E	O	R	O	L	L	M	L	W	O	S
R	A	W	T	M	W	A	S	F	S	I	E	P	E	S	M	H
L	W	O	O	P	C	O	L	O	P	I	T	A	L	A	T	I
H	H	H	W	O	N	O	P	P	W	E	P	E	N	A	S	O
P	T	S	E	O	S	C	E	A	G	M	A	T	B	O	W	T
B	U	E	L	S	M	R	E	P	T	E	P	E	T	O	A	C
C	O	T	T	O	N	S	W	A	B	E	E	E	C	C	S	I
R	M	H	S	P	O	N	G	E	P	I	R	A	P	O	H	O
N	H	T	O	O	T	H	P	A	S	T	E	A	A	M	S	M
T	O	O	W	T	T	O	O	A	S	I	U	P	T	B	E	G

TOOTHPASTE

TISSUE

SPONGE

TOOTHBRUSH

COTTON SWAB

#Summary

Puberty is normal and a healthy part of your development. It can be exciting and confusing at the same time. Your body will change, and it may be uncomfortable but just know that it is absolutely necessary for you to reproduce later on in life. It is important for you to know what's happening to your body so that you are prepared for the changes that will come. Embrace puberty as much as you can and don't be afraid to ask questions BRUH!

Now that you know a thing or two about puberty, how would you describe puberty in your own words?

_____

_____

_____

_____

_____

_____

_____

_____

_____

_____

What changes have you noticed in your body since you started puberty?

_____

_____

_____

_____

_____

_____

_____

What change do you like the most and why?

_____

_____

_____

_____

_____

_____

_____

What change do you not like and why?

_____

_____

_____

_____

_____

_____

_____

#MyThoughts

MY GUIDE TO BECOMING A MAN

BOOK 2

Table Of Contents

 # #Self Esteem

What do you think self-esteem is?

_____

_____

_____

According to Webster's Dictionary if we break down the word this is what we get.

Self: You + Esteem: Respect and Admiration

If you put these words together, how you respect and admire yourself is the true definition of self-esteem. It's how you feel about yourself, your confidence, your identity, your morals and how you respect yourself. Now that your body is changing you are going to start paying more attention to it and if you look good, you'll feel good. This means that you have to take really good care of your body (stay healthy, eat well, and keep yourself nice and clean). Puberty may make some of your body parts look weird at first, don't focus too much on what looks weird, rather focus on the things you like about your body. For example:

1. Ask your parents to take you to the barber for a fresh haircut when you need it cut. If you wear braids, ask your parents to get your hair rebraided often so that it always looks nice. Believe it or not this will make you look better and maybe even feel better.

2. Your clothes don't have to be brand new to look good, but they should be neat and clean. Ask your parents to wash your clothes often so you'll always feel and look good when you put them on.

There are so many other ways you can feel good about yourself during this awkward stage of puberty.

What do you think are some other things you can do to feel good about yourself?

_____

_____

_____

You should be the ONLY person that makes you feel good. You should always be confident in who you are! Esteem is also knowing what your strengths and weaknesses are. Use your strengths to make you a better version of yourself but be mindful of the areas that you need to work on for growth. You are not perfect, and you do not need to be. You just need to be happy and comfortable with yourself.

Pause for a minute and think about 3 things that make you happy about yourself?

1._____

2._____

3._____

What is low self-esteem?

Having low self-esteem is terrible Bruh 😡. Almost anything can cause you to have low self-esteem, (lack of confidence, life experiences, traumatic experiences, feelings of being unloved or unwanted, etc). Any of these triggers can cause you to ignore and block the positive qualities about yourself. You may even put yourself down and use negative words to describe yourself or even begin to feel inferior to others! We may all go through this at some time in our lives, but what matters the most is not staying in this terrible space.

What would you like to work on to make yourself a better you?

_____

_____

_____

What is healthy self-esteem?

If you suffer from low self-esteem my heart goes out to you, but there are several ways you can turn this around Bruh. You don't have to stay in this place. You are a king so I want you to talk to yourself like a king. Come on, let's try it. Repeat after me, *"I am strong and I can do anything if I put my mind to it and work hard for it!"* I hope you felt better when you said that to yourself. Repeat this to yourself when you feel down and I hope it changes the way you feel. If that does work, here are a few confidence boosters if you need them.

- Talk positive to yourself Bruh. You are handsome, you are intelligent and you're a cool dude, don't forget that! 👊

- Please, please, please STOP renting out the space in your head and harboring negative thoughts. You're gonna have a serious headache if you do that! Always think positive.
- Encourage yourself. Get outta your feelings and root for yourself Bruh!
- Acknowledge your strengths and make a list. Bruh, there are so many good things about you, you're awesome!
- Stop procrastinating and make some goals. You gotta start somewhere so let's get it moving!
- Get a hobby or do something you're passionate about. These things will help build up your confidence, believe it or not.
- Talk to a counselor or therapist. Learn from them, they can help you with self-management skills and techniques to help boost your confidence. I think everyone should have a therapist, get you one Bruh, it will change your life! Seeing a therapist doesn't make you crazy or weird, it says you value your feelings and that is always a good thing.

What are your values?

Think about your values. What are a few values that are important to you as a young guy?

_____

_____

_____

_____

Values are important as you become a man….. why? Because having values such as self- confidence and integrity can lead to healthy relationships and your personal growth which is important as you become a man. This identity can empower you to set healthy boundaries, make better life choices, and foster respect from others Bruh!

Take a moment to think about why you're a cool dude😎.

Fill in the boxes with some cool things about yourself.

#MoodSwings - My Emotions

Going through puberty is tough and it can be so uncomfortable for some guys. All the physical and emotional changes can seem like a roller coaster ride, you may even think you're going crazy 🙀 a little. These feelings are normal and unfortunately all a part of your transition to manhood. We tend to focus a lot on the physical changes your body goes through and not so much the emotional feelings which are equally important. Well, Testosterone (the male hormone) that is responsible for these body changes are also responsible for the shift in your mood swings and emotions 😭.

Due to the hormonal changes you're experiencing, some young men may notice a change in their confidence, feelings and/or emotions about a lot of things. Feelings about your family, friends and even yourself may change. You may be more sensitive towards certain things and/or people and not know how to process these feelings. For example, one day you may feel really happy 😃 and then a few minutes later you're angry 😡 and don't want to be around anyone. You're not going crazy, you're just growing up, and your body is trying to adjust to the hormonal imbalance you're going through. As you get older it will change and if not you'll learn how to process and deal with these feelings and emotions. If you get so angry that you feel like you're going to explode, take a minute to calm yourself down. It's ok to walk away or be quiet for a minute. This does NOT make you a punk. What this means is that you're learning how to control your anger as well as your actions.

Sometimes when your body is physically out of whack, this can cause a change in your emotions as well. For example, if you're not eating well (junk food more than healthy foods) this can throw your hormones off 🤮. You become irritable and moody, and this can definitely affect your emotions.

Being lazy and stagnant can also mess up your emotions and moods. Get up and move around Bruh. Be active and get a hobby. Exercising can really boost your emotions and self-esteem, and it makes you feel better physically, which is good for your health. Make sure to get plenty of rest too especially during puberty. These changes are happening faster than you can imagine and your body, believe it or not, needs a good night's rest.

What's your thoughts:

_____

_____

_____

_____

_____

_____

_____

_____

_____

_____

_____

_____

#MySexuality

At some point during puberty, you'll start to question your identity as a male and what it is that you like or dislike and who you are becoming (your identity) which is important to you. This involves your feelings about who you are attracted to. Sometimes these feelings are overwhelming and confusing, but they are normal and eventually you will figure it out.

Let's define Sexuality

Sexuality is your feelings and attraction towards someone (young men or young women) in a physical, emotional or sexual way. It's not just about sex though, it involves how you identify, how you understand and express your feelings in respectful relationships.

Sex education most times is limited to adolescent males and females. Rarely does it focus on a boy's pleasure with other boys and their relationships. In this journal, I wanted to give this topic a safe space for you to discuss how you may feel if this relates to you. It can be really hard to process these feelings though and you may need to talk to someone (maybe a therapist or trusted adult). Feelings of being isolated, embarrassed or looked down on after "coming out" can change and/or affect your life if you're not able to process these feelings in a positive way.

Love is love and who you love and wish to be with is your choice Bruh! If you're interested in boys that may not necessarily mean that you are gay and being interested in girls doesn't mean you're straight. It means that during puberty these thoughts and attractions are heightened and can be intense for some guys. These thoughts are a way for you to sort out your sexual feelings and that's ok.

Think about your sexuality, what does it mean to you?

_____

_____

_____

_____

_____

_____

_____

I found some questions online that I wanted to include in this journal. I thought about the young fellas who are struggling with this. These questions DO NOT define who you are but rather make you think about your feelings if you're unsure of your identity. These questions can be found at

https://www.wikihow.com/Relationships/Sexuality-Quiz

1. Do you ever fantasize about being intimate with someone of the same gender as you?

    A. Yes, I do fantasize about that regularly.

    B. Yes, but rarely.

    C. No, I never do. It doesn't seem appealing to me.

    D. I'm not sure.

2. How would you feel if someone of the opposite gender leaned in to kiss you?

    A. I'd be aroused and really excited to kiss them back.

    B. I think I'd be interested, but I'm not totally sure.

C. I'd be uncomfortable and not interested.

D. I'm not sure.

3. Whose bodies (girls or boys) do you pay the most attention to when watching movies and shows?

A. People of the same gender as me.

B. People of the opposite gender as me.

C. People of both genders.

D. I don't usually pay any attention to people's bodies in the media I watch.

5. If an attractive person of the same gender started hitting on you, how would you feel?

A. Excited and even aroused.

B. Curious to explore where it leads.

C. Definitely uninterested.

D. I'm not sure.

6. Does the idea of hanging out with another guy seem sexually appealing?

A. Yes, I've enjoyed that experience in the past. I would love that.

B. I've never had that experience before, but I'm definitely curious to see if I like it.

C. No, I don't want to hang out with someone of the same gender.

D. I'm not sure.

7. At a party, who would you enjoy flirting with all night?

   A. Someone of the same gender.

   B. Someone of the opposite gender.

   C. Either gender sounds great.

   D. Someone I like, but I probably wouldn't want the flirting to lead to anything more than that.

8. When you think of physical attraction and intimacy, which gender comes to mind first?

   A. My gender.

   B. The opposite gender.

   C. It depends—sometimes it's my gender and other times it's the opposite.

   D. No one (or, unsure).

9. Do you find guys and girls equally attractive?

   A. No, I find guys much more attractive.

   B. No, I find girls a lot more attractive.

   C. Yes, I find both to be equally attractive, or at least it's close.

   D. I'm not attracted to either gender.

There is no score to these questions. The purpose of these questions is to help you if you are struggling with your identity.

#V-Card aka My Virginity

Do you know what a virgin is?   Circle YES or NO.

If you circled YES tell me why that is?

_____

_____

_____

_____

According to Merriam-Webster, "A virgin is a person who has NOT had sexual intercourse." Some would describe sex as the penis penetrating the vagina. Choosing to have sex (losing your virginity) for the first time is a big deal. If and when you choose to have sex make sure that it is something you want to do and not pressured into doing. Your consent is needed 100% of the time, remember that.

 If you are a virgin, there is absolutely no reason for you to be ashamed. The fact that you're a virgin means that you've probably thought about all the things that could go wrong if you were not prepared and that's a smart way to think. Stay in control, don't be pressured into having sex, take your time, and move at your own pace. Don't have sex until you are absolutely ready, it's not a race. Besides, once you start having sex, you may feel different emotionally. Sex should be a special connection between two responsible people. Here are some questions you should take into consideration when it comes to having sex for the first time.

1. Have you had a conversation about sex with the other person?

2. Is this person someone you consider worthy enough to share your body with?

3. What are you going to use to prevent an unwanted pregnancy and/or a sexually transmitted infection?

4. Is the environment a safe place to have sex?

5. Have you guys visited the clinic to make sure you're both negative of STI's?

My Thoughts

_____

_____

_____

_____

_____

_____

_____

_____

_____

#FeelingMyself

Masturbation

Masturbation can be a very uncomfortable conversation for some guys to talk about. The truth is that most people do it! Now that your body has begun to transform, masturbation allows you to learn your anatomy (your body) as well as detect when or if something is going on in your body.

According to Webster's Dictionary, "masturbation is sexual stimulation of one's own genitals for sexual arousal or other sexual pleasure, usually to the point of orgasm". The stimulation may involve hands, fingers, objects, sex toys. It is the act of enjoying self-pleasure without feeling guilt or shame.

You are probably asking yourself if masturbation is normal? The truth is that it may be for some and perfectly fine for others. If I can be transparent, masturbation is a part of your sexuality. It is perfectly okay to touch your body, after all it belongs to you and it's yours. Touching your body in a pleasurable way allows you to understand what makes you feel good. Masturbating can help you to relieve life related stressors and most importantly it's safe.

My Feelings/ Questions / Concerns about masturbation:

_____

_____

#ControlYourselfBruh

Abstinence

Is dry humping, kissing and /or cuddling with someone you like considered abstinence (avoiding) behavior?

What do you think and why

_____

_____

_____

_____

Sexual abstinence is a decision and the practice of choosing NOT to engage in sexual activity (vaginal penetration, anal penetration and or oral sex.) It is a way to avoid the many risks that come with sex. This decision can help you to stay focused on your school studies, future goals and things that are important to you in your life.

Abstinence is the best practice for birth control as per, MsThomasRN because it prevents an unwanted pregnancy. It also prevents you from coming in contact with any sexually transmitted infections. Abstinence takes LOTS of control because during puberty the change in your hormones can cause you to be very curious about your sexual feelings. Plus peer pressure from your friends can be #CRAZY! It's easy to get "caught up" because you want to be a part of the "cool guys" but staying focused is even cooler, don't do it yet Bruh!

What are your thoughts on abstinence and how do you feel remaining abstinent until you are older and mentally mature to have sex?

_____

_____

_____

_____

_____

Have you ever been pressured into having sex with someone? If so, how did you handle/cope with that?

_____

_____

_____

_____

_____

#Smash

Sex

Let's start with this question. What do you think the purpose of sex is?

_____

_____

_____

_____

_____

_____

The biblical purpose of sex is for a male and female to reproduce. Others may say the purpose of sex is to relieve sexual stress. The answer to this question is different for everyone. Some guys may be ready as teenagers and others as older men. Some may not want to ever have sex and that's ok. It's all up to you and how comfortable you feel about it. Making the decision to have sex for the first time can be overwhelming and difficult. Whatever decision you make, your decision should be YOUR choice and you should not be PRESSURED or FORCED into having sex with anyone without your consent. Sex involves physical, mental and emotional feelings with the other person. There are many important decisions and responsibilities that come with having sex and if you're not prepared to make these decisions, it's probably best that you wait until you are.

If you are having doubts about your decision, you're probably not ready. Let's be clear, having a DESIRE to have sex is not the same as being PREPARED to have sex.

What are your thoughts about Sex?

_____

_____

_____

_____

_____

_____

_____

_____

_____

_____

Before you decide to have sex, ask yourself if you have all the information you need about sex. Here are a few questions to think about:

1. How well do I know this person and do I really want to have sex with them?
2. How do I protect my health from possible disease?
3. Am I knowledgeable about safe sex and condom use?
4. What happens if the condom breaks?
5. Will sex be painful the first time
6. Am I comfortable with someone seeing me naked and touching my body?

These questions are important to your physical health and should be very important for you to consider in your decision. If you were uncomfortable asking yourself or answering any of these questions maybe you should really take some time to think about your decision and you should probably WAIT to have sex.

Choosing to be sexually active is a decision that is very important, and it can affect the rest of your life especially if you make the wrong decision. If you decide to become sexually active, I highly recommend you protect yourself from unwanted pregnancy and disease. Protecting yourself during sex can allow you to enjoy sex especially when you are responsible and ready. Protecting yourself means a few things:

Choose the right partner. Bruh, just because he/she "looks good" doesn't mean they are good for you!

The person that you decide to have your first sexual relationship with should be someone that is special to you. It should be someone that you care about and someone that you trust with your mind, your heart, and your body. Make sure that you are mentally, emotionally and physically okay with your decision.

Once you and your partner have decided to have sex, both of you should visit the local clinic and both of you should be screened and tested for any sexually transmitted infections prior to having sex. Just know, the right person will be okay with this, remember his or her health is just as important. Just because you get tested and are given negative results does not mean that you still shouldn't use condoms. It just means that if the condom breaks or it falls off, you and your partner will not come in contact with any sexually transmitted infections, because you are both clear of any of those.

Once you have been tested, your next step should be to get condoms. If you choose to have sex with a female, it's a good idea that she starts birth control. Birth control plus condoms adds a double layer of protection against diseases and unwanted pregnancy.

If you have decided to have sex keep in mind that sex can be uncomfortable or may seem weird, are you prepared for that?

Here are some more questions about sex for you to think about:

Are you or any of your friends having sex? If so, how does this make you

feel?

_____

_____

Have you ever been asked to watch porn (people having sex with each other) and if so, how do you feel about that? If not, what was your reaction to this question?

_____

_____

_____

_____

How would you react if someone you liked asked you to have sex with them?

_____

_____

_____

_____

Are there any questions you are uncomfortable with when it comes to sex?

_____

_____

_____

_____

#KnockedUp

Pregnancy

How does pregnancy happen Bruh?

In order for a female to get pregnant your sperm must connect with her egg. Simply put, when you have unprotected sex and ejaculate your sperm into a female's body (her vagina) it is possible for you to create a pregnancy. Of the millions of sperms you produce it ONLY takes 1 sperm for this to happen. This is why safe sex is very important.

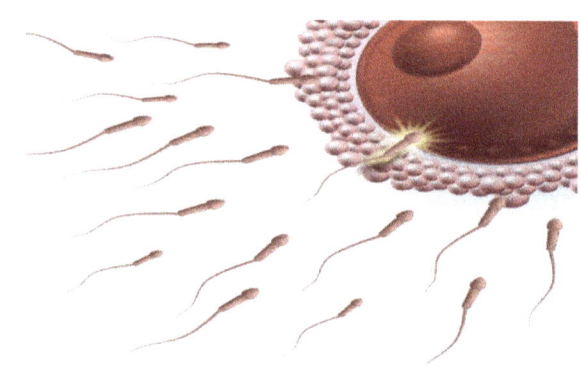

_____

_____

_____

_____

Is it possible to get a girl pregnant during puberty?

When boys and girls go through puberty, both of your bodies are preparing themselves for reproduction (make a baby). Girls start their menstrual cycle (period) and boys have wet dreams and start to ejaculate semen and sperm. This means that even during puberty you can get a female pregnant.

How do I prevent an unwanted pregnancy?

In order to prevent an unwanted pregnancy it is VERY important for you to use condoms. Condoms (if used correctly and ALL the time) can prevent your semen from entering a female's body (vagina) during sex. Making sure that the female you are with is on some type of birth control also helps to prevent an unwanted pregnancy. Condoms + Birth Control = Safe Sex.

shutterstock.com · 104044550

_____

_____

_____

#Condoms

The most popular type of birth control is a condom. If used correctly it can provide protection against unwanted pregnancy and sexually transmitted infections. Most clinics, schools and community-based programs provide condoms for free but if you had to purchase them, they are accessible and available in most stores. Condoms are applied to the male penis; it also is your responsibility to make sure that you have them available when needed and that they are put on correctly. Condoms should be used EVERY TIME you have sex.

Do some research and write down a few places here where you can get free condoms if you need them?

HOW TO USE MALE CONDOM

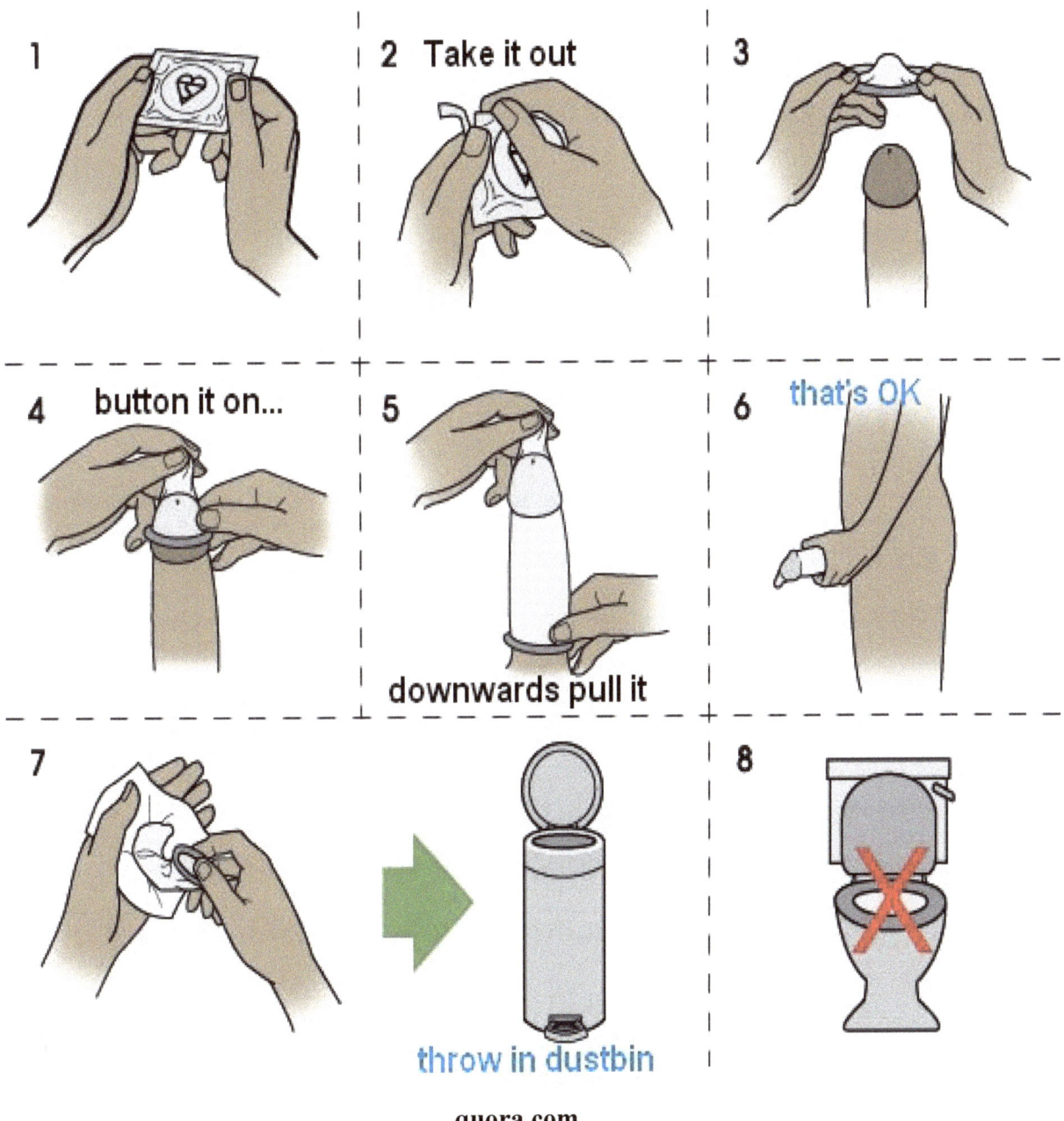

1

2 Take it out

3

4 button it on...

5 downwards pull it

6 that's OK

7

throw in dustbin

8

quora.com

69

#Don'tTrustItBruh!

Now that you know you can reproduce and make a baby NEVER EVER EVER have unprotected sex if you're not ready to become a parent. Even if she tells you she's on birth control USE CONDOMS anyway. I've heard many guys say "sex feels better without a condom and if you pull out real quick, she won't get pregnant"... 🙄. Bruh let's talk.

Pull Out Game

The pull-out method is also known as the withdrawal method. This means that during sex the guy will pull his penis out of the vagina right before he ejaculates. In doing this he hopes to not get any semen and sperm into the woman's vagina so that she does not get pregnant. The pull out method has the highest failure of all the birth control methods and is not a good choice in preventing an unwanted pregnancy.

According to the Cleveland Clinic, about 1/ 5 people who use withdrawal will become pregnant every year. Don't trust it Bruh! Use condoms ALL THE TIME! The pull out method also DOES NOT protect you from getting a sexually transmitted infection and that's double trouble. 🤮

Birth control is the responsibility of the guy as well and the gal. For guys condoms are your best choice. For girls, they have more options, here are a few you can suggest to her if she is not aware, she'll be really impressed that you know this too, you can thank me later...lol

Birth Control Methods for Women

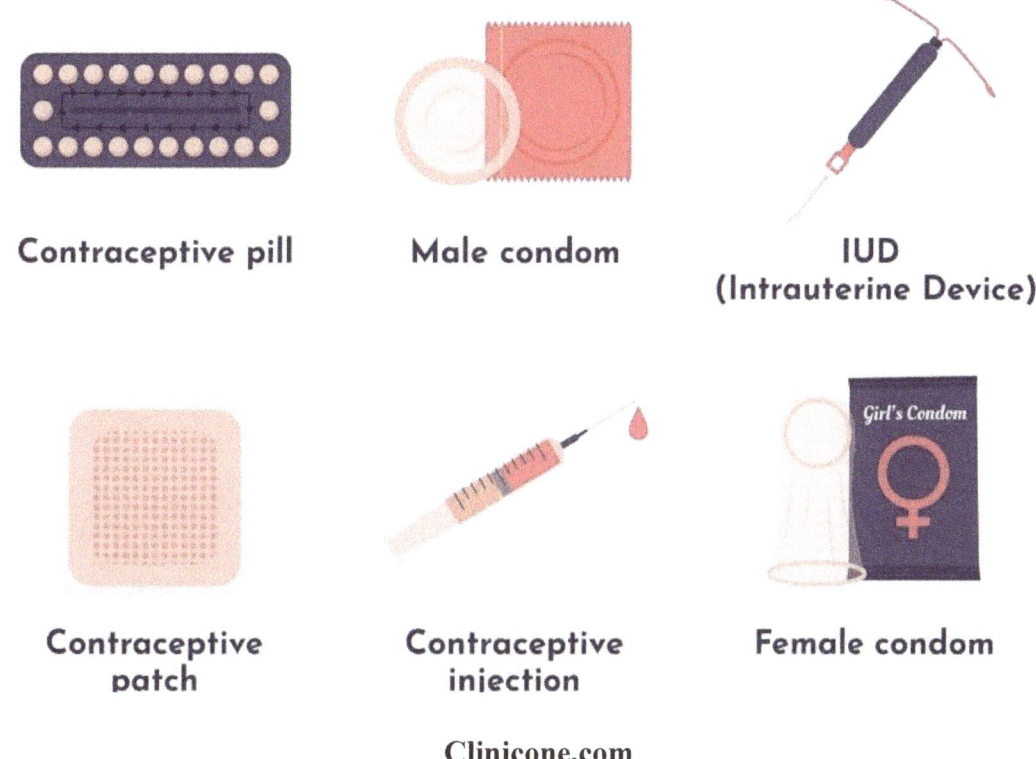

Contraceptive pill   Male condom   IUD
(Intrauterine Device)

Contraceptive
patch   Contraceptive
injection   Female condom

Clinicone.com

If a girl who you were about to have sex with told you she was on birth control
and that you did not need to use condoms, what would you say and what would
you do?

_____

_____

_____

#Emergency Contraception aka Plan B

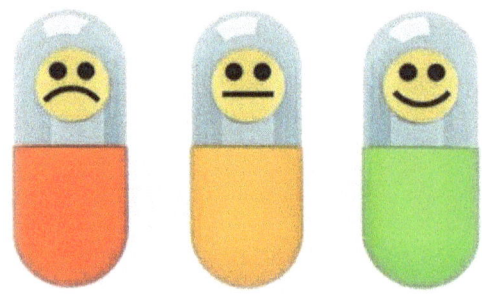

What happens if the condom breaks or comes off during sex? What would you do?

_____

_____

_____

If you panic first, this would be understandable. Sometimes condoms do break and /or come off. If this happens and the young lady you are with is not on birth control it may be possible for her to get pregnant if any semen and sperm got into her vagina. Don't panic, here's what you can do. Go to the local pharmacy and ask for Emergency Contraception (Plan B) or (the morning after pill). This is a pill that can be used to prevent an unwanted pregnancy. Plan B is emergency contraception that is only intended for emergency use if taken with 120 hours (5 days) of unprotected or failed birth control use. This medication is NOT to be used as a birth control method; it will NOT work the same. Plan B can be purchased over the counter without a prescription and is available in most pharmacies.

My Thoughts

_____

_____

_____

_____

_____

_____

_____

_____

_____

_____

_____

#YouBuggin

Sexually Transmitted Infections

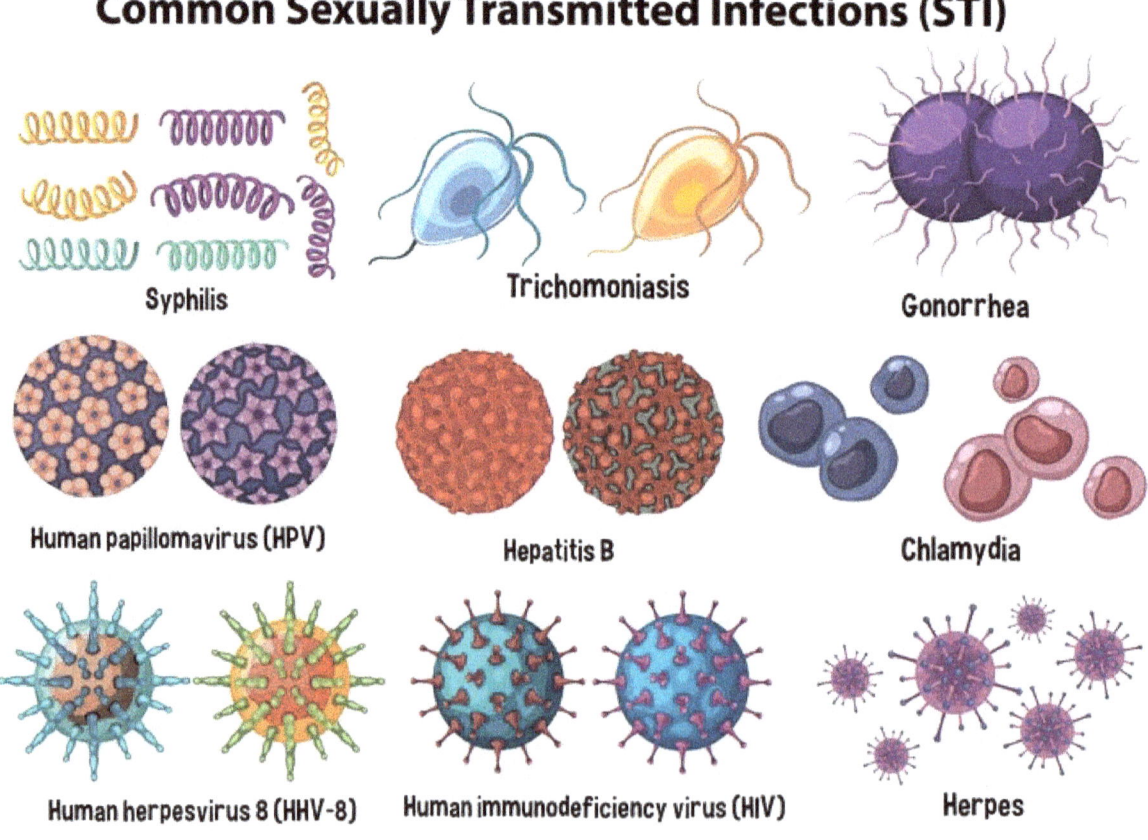

freepik.com

A sexually transmitted infection (STI) is an infection that you get from a person who already has an infection during sex. Most times you won't know if a person is infected because the person may not have any visual symptoms. Sometimes they do not even know they are infected. Therefore, it is VERY important to protect your health and wear condoms if you are going to be sexually active.

There are some STI's that are treatable and there are some that are not. They can affect your reproductive system, causing challenges and/or complications bearing children when you are ready. Let's talk about a few of these STI's.

Sexually Transmitted Infections that are Curable

Chlamydia is a common STI that can cause infection among both men and women. It can cause permanent damage to a woman's reproductive system. This can make it difficult or impossible to get pregnant if it's not treated.

Gonorrhea is another common STI. It affects the mucous membranes of the reproductive tract, including the cervix, uterus, and the fallopian tubes in women and the urethra in women and men.

Syphilis is a bacterial infection usually spread by sexual contact. It starts as a painless sore. The most common symptom may include a rash on the palms of the hands and the soles of the feet. Symptoms come and go but it is treatable with antibiotics.

Pubic Lice is commonly called "crabs". They are tiny insects found in the genital area and they can cause itching and irritation. They are treated with a special shampoo and shaving of your genital area.

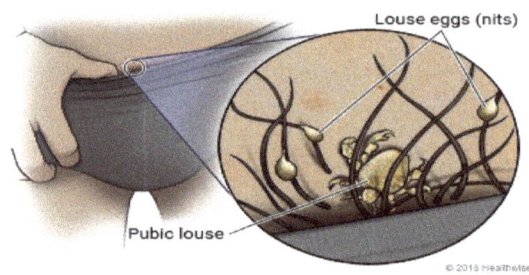

Scabies is a very contagious, and itchy skin condition caused by a tiny burrowing mite. They spread quickly through close physical contact.

Sexually Transmitted Infections that are NOT Curable

According to the World Health Organization **"Human Immunodeficiency Virus" (HIV)** is an infection that attacks the body's immune system. Acquired immunodeficiency syndrome (AIDS) is the most advanced stage of the disease.

HIV targets the body's white blood cells, weakening the immune system. This makes it easier to get sick with diseases like tuberculosis, infections and some cancers.

HIV is spread from the body fluids of an infected person, including blood, semen and vaginal fluids. It is not spread by kisses, hugs or sharing food. It can also spread from a mother to her baby.

HIV can be treated and prevented with antiretroviral therapy (ART). Untreated HIV can progress to AIDS, often after many years."

Not everyone will have signs or symptoms of HIV/AIDS but those who do can have some of the symptoms below.

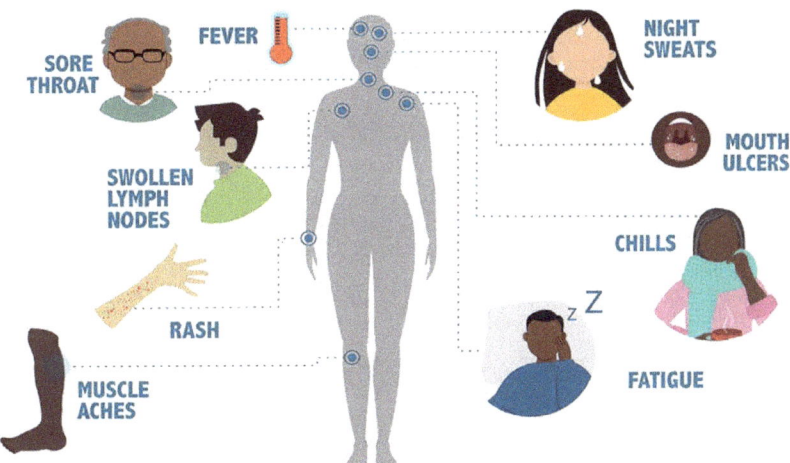

Centers for Disease Control

HIV/AIDS is a deadly disease. If you are going to be sexually active PLEASE PLEASE PLEASE use condoms ALL OF THE TIME!!!!! Although there is no cure, HIV/AIDS is PREVENTABLE! Protect yourself and your body.

Your Thoughts on Sexually Transmitted Infections:

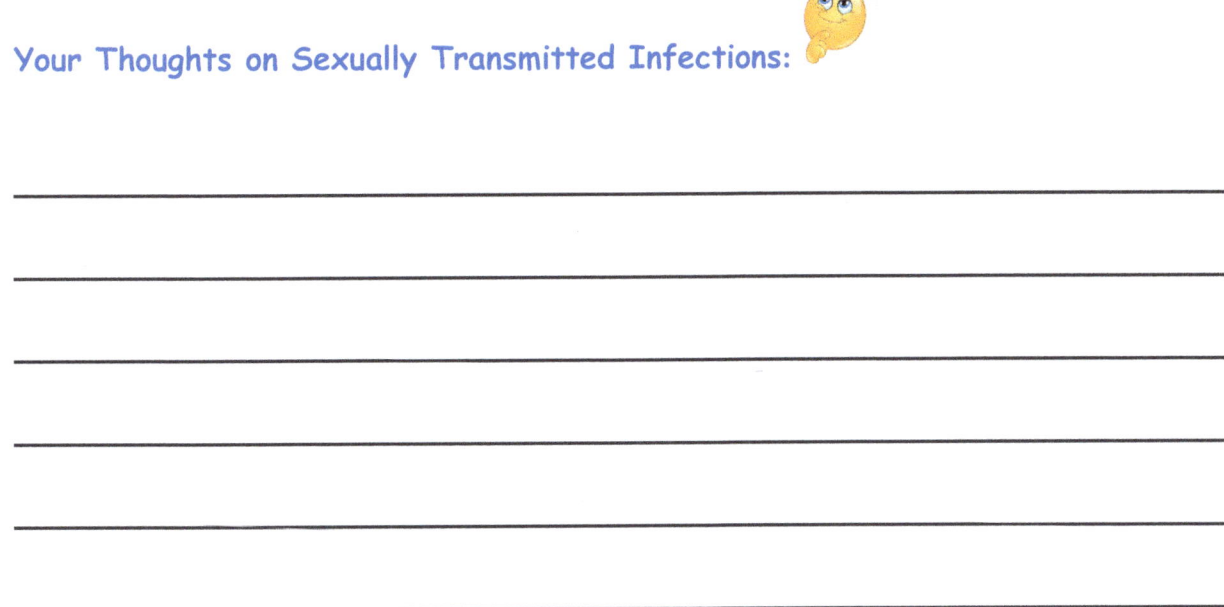

_____

_____

_____

_____

_____

_____

Herpes is a STI that is spread during sex if you come in contact with an infected person's sores, blisters, body fluids and/ or skin. Once the virus enters your body, it will remain there FOREVER. Occasionally it will manifest itself as a blister or cold sore on your body. It can be extremely painful especially in the penis area. There are two types of herpes and both are equally contagious:

1. **Oral Herpes aka a cold sore is seen on your lip and is often contagious during kissing and /or oral sex. It is physically unpleasant to look at but fortunately it is temporary and can go away with medication.**

2. **Gential Herpes is spread through sexual contact with someone that is infected. Medication can reduce the amount of outbreaks you'll have BUT……. Herpes is a LIFELONG infection which means even when you don't have symptoms, the virus will ALWAYS remain in your body.**

To prevent Herpes infection, you should always use condoms, limit the amount of people you have sex with and most important AVOID having sex with someone if you see ANY genital sores on their body. Here is a picture of what herpes looks like.

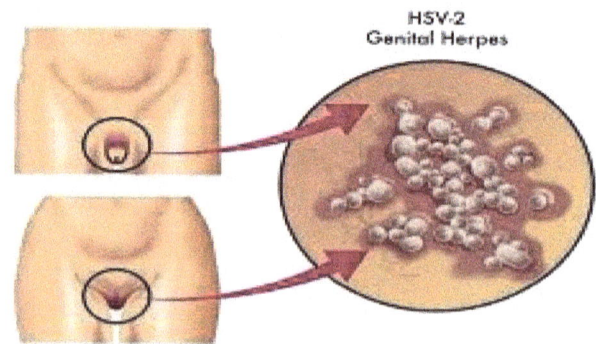

diag.vn/en/std/genital-herpes/l

#PERIODT
Girls and Puberty

Only females and males can mate and reproduce with each other. In order for the human race to continue it is necessary for human beings to procreate. Now that you understand your body and its importance, understanding the female human body is equally important for this reason.

Although this journal is for you it is important to know what girls go through during puberty. When both of you get older you will need each other in order to reproduce (make a baby). So here is some informative information for you.

Just like you girls go through puberty at an early age and many changes happen in their body as well. These changes are due to the female hormone called "Estrogen". Just like boys, girls are born with reproductive organs, a vagina. The anatomy of their body is much different from yours.

Female reproductive system
Internal and external

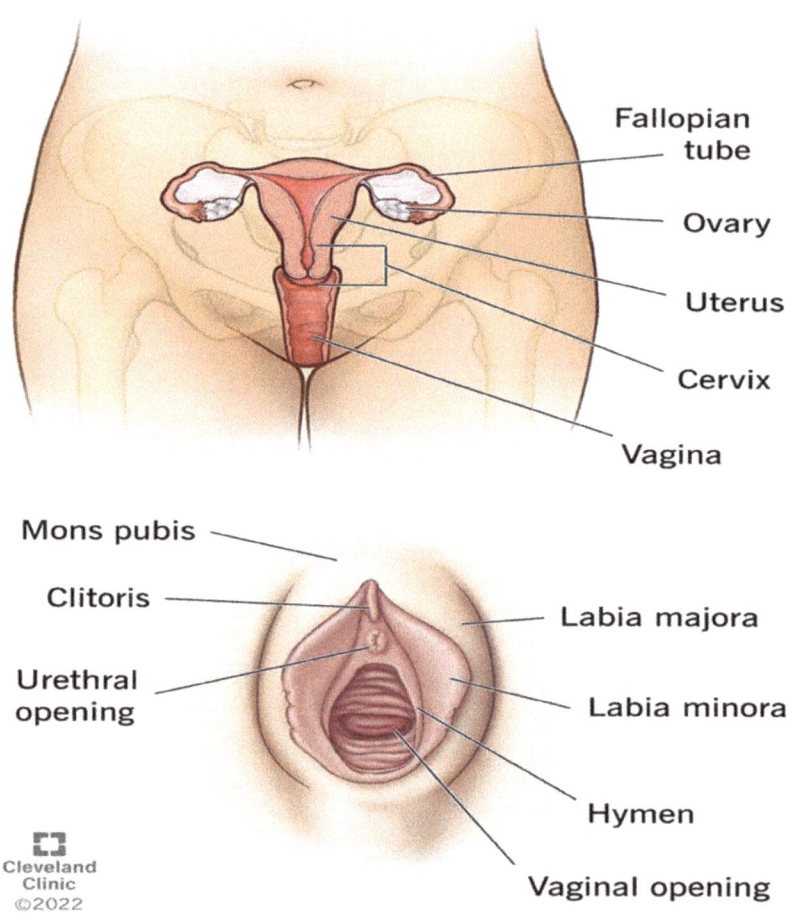

The vagina is a very sensitive organ in the female's body. Its purpose is to receive semen and sperm from the male's penis during sex to produce a baby. The diagram below shows the stages of development and maturity a female goes through when puberty starts.

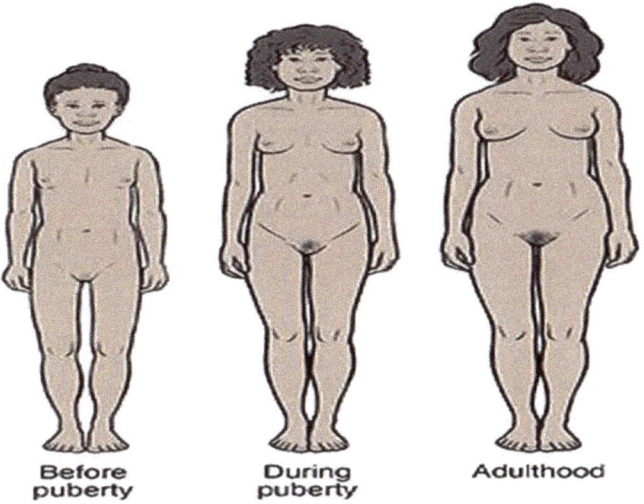

Before puberty   During puberty   Adulthood

Physical changes in girls usually start around age 10 years old. Here are some of those changes that she will go through during puberty.

Breast "buds" start to form   Acne first appears   Armpit and pubic hair starts to grow

You experience a growth spurt   You start your period

Flo App.com

Females are an important part of the reproduction cycle. Just like you, they experience mood swings, acne, peer pressure and may be sexually active. Knowing how the male body operates is important for you to know as well, Bruh!

#Summary

Hey Bruh,

Let me start by saying you are a cool dude! Puberty is scary and it will be an uncomfortable time in your life. You are going to question your appearance, your moods, and your thoughts, but do your best to embrace the changes and make the RIGHT choices. You will be tempted to go against your morals and your beliefs, stay strong! You don't need to participate in any behavior that makes you uncomfortable just so that you can fit in with the "Other Fellas". Focus on what's really important like your educational and life goals. These goals will take you further than those dudes.

I wrote this book because I wanted to be intentional about empowering you as you transition into this phase of your life. Having a healthy conversation about puberty is important to your health and wellbeing and it will help you deal with the changes positively and may help you feel secure. Puberty is normal and a natural part of growing into the awesome dude you will become. Remember to always empower and

invest in yourself and NEVER EVER EVER be ashamed of who you are. BRUH!

MsThomasRN

#MyThoughts

Safe Sex

```
K U X Y O Y O A U M H S F E M A L E C O N D O M
G V T G P L R K A Z D E L Y S W M Y T K I S N Q
I U W R H S C Y B A P Q L E Y K H H M Z X R N T
R B A K E K H O B S P O I C I N Y Q Z Y Z F F B
K V D R C Q Y K Z N D I P J A H H Y B Q U Q P F
C M P U G H Y E L K P A E E S M O D N O C T F B
I O O G V B R T U A L P H R G D M T M A B L L N
X Y N Q F X R V N E H N T T I K L R T M C E J U
H K J T T T U L Y E C S A F E S E X O V X X B K
I P T V R E W D L H O Q Y U P E G I V X R P N V
V D A S B A B U F O I S M Y C A M R A H P F U G
X W Z F T C C W V E Y D D O Q N Y A A J Y E V U
G B E Q O H C E H Y Z M W M O D M I D W B I R C
I H B H F L F E P Q O T A I I N R P E Y J T H L
D P C D N A V X S T L V T G N L D X D F D H S E
I I E J I M X X J G I A A X O J D Q Y R P U G N
W C Q J Q Y Y D S O C O O H M N S G W Y N K U B
M N V X H D Y V P I C V N N Q T O K O X V Z C E
I Q I D N I B S N F V H H Y G B P M D T E Y A Z
T A Y Y U A Y U S B M R S O T S E G W D L C U T
S T X F L N M R K J H F N V N Y U R X Q K Q C K
P A Q E F M N Y U F X M I P A T J D A K L T D F
Z N G X O U F Z S W E C O N S E N T G M O O N M
N B U C R I U H E R P E S B T W E E M E S P L E
```

Contraception	Female Condom	Communication
Chlamydia	Monogamy	Pharmacy
The pill	Safe sex	Consent
Condoms	Herpes	HIV
STI	GP	

wordmint.com

Male Reproductive System

Across

3. Seminal vesicle fluid is _____, which helps neutralize the acidity of the vaginal tract, prolonging the lifespan of sperm.

5. _____ is the process by which haploid spermatozoa develop from germ cells in the seminiferous tubules of the testis.

9. _____ is necessary for sperm production (spermatogenesis).

12. The vas deferens joins with the seminal vesicle to form the _____ duct, which passes through the prostate and empties into the urethra.

14. Composition of semen is primarily from the secretions of the prostate gland, epididymis, _____ vesicles, testes, and bulbourethral glands.

15. Semen is milky-white fluid containing sperm cells and secretions from the _____ glands.

16. _____ is the stage of spermatogenesis wherein the spermatids differentiate into mature spermatozoa.

17. The accessory sex glands produce _____ fluid and clean and lubricate the urethra.

18. The primary hormones in the functioning of the male reproductive system are follicle-stimulating hormone (FSH), luteinizing hormone (LH), and _____.

19. The paired testes produce both sperm and _____, the hormones that support male reproductive physiology.

20. The prostate gland enhances _____ of sperm.

Down

1. The seminal vesicle helps _____ sperm.

2. Sperm are the male _____ produced in the seminiferous tubules of the testes.

4. The function of the male reproductive system is to produce _____ and transfer them to the female reproductive system.

6. _____ is important in the development of male characteristics, including muscle mass and strength, fat distribution, bone mass, and sex drive.

7. _____ stimulates the production of testosterone, which is necessary to continue the process of spermatogenesis.

8. Usually, the developing spermatogonia cells remain connected by cytoplasmic bridges, until they have formed mature _____.

10. The _____ receives immature sperm from the testis and stores them as they mature.

11. The _____ glands function to lubricate the spongy urethra for the passage of the ejaculate.

13. The prostate contains _____ muscles that help expel semen during ejaculation.

Explore the full series by MsThomasRN

Give your son or daughter real, relatable, and medically accurate guidance from a certified Reproductive Health & Sexuality Educator who keeps it honest and empowering.